Standards and Special Educational Needs

Also available from Continuum:

Peter Benton and Tim O'Brien: *Special Needs and the Beginning Teacher*
Paul Croll and Diana Moses: *Special Needs in the Primary School*
Hannah Mortimer: *Special Needs and Early Years Provision*
Tim O'Brien and Denis Guiney: *Differentiation in Teaching and Learning*

STANDARDS AND SPECIAL EDUCATIONAL NEEDS

The Importance of Standards
of Pupil Achievement

Michael Farrell

CONTINUUM
London and New York

Continuum

The Tower Building
11 York Road
London SE1 7NX

370 Lexington Avenue
New York
NY 10017-6503

First published 2001

British Library Cataloguing-in-Publication Data
A catalogue record for this book is available from the British Library.

ISBN 0-8264-5432-1 (hardback)
   0-8264-5431-3 (paperback)

Typeset by Paston PrePress Ltd, Beccles, Suffolk
Printed and bound in Great Britain by Biddles Ltd, *www.biddles.co.uk*

Contents

About the author

Michael Farrell trained as a teacher and as a psychologist and has served as a headteacher, a lecturer at the Institute of Education, London, and a local authority education inspector for special education. He has managed national projects for both City University and the Department for Education.

Michael Farrell presently works as a special education consultant in Britain and abroad. This has included policy development and training with local education authorities, work with voluntary organizations, support to schools in the independent sector and advice to the State Bureau of Foreign Experts, China and the Ministry of Education, Seychelles. He has lectured widely in the United Kingdom and abroad.

Author of over two hundred articles on education and psychology, Michael Farrell has edited thirty educational books. Among his other publications are *The Handbook of Education* (Blackwell, 1996) with Kerry and Kerry, *Key Issues for Primary Schools* (Routledge, 1999), *Key Issues for Secondary Schools* (Routledge, 2001) and *The Special Education Handbook* (David Fulton, 1997, 1998, 2000).

Acknowledgements

The following colleagues commented on earlier drafts of the book or parts of it: Mr Gerry Ackroyd, Senior Educational Psychologist, Education, Youth and Leisure Services, London Borough of Hillingdon, England; Dr Rob Ashdown, Headteacher, St Luke's School, North Lincolnshire, England; Professor Philip Garner, Nottingham Trent University, England; Mrs Pat Locke, Headteacher, Christchurch Church of England Infant School, Surrey, England; Mr David Tully, Finance Manager, Education, Youth and Leisure Services, London Borough of Hillingdon, England.

I am most grateful to these colleagues. Their assistance does not imply that their views are the same as those expressed in the text. The views expressed in *Standards and Special Educational Need*s are my own. Any shortcomings of the book are of course entirely my own.

Introduction

Readers of this book

In *The History of Tom Jones, a Foundling*, Henry Fielding embraces as well as anyone before or since the point of introducing the reader to what he might expect in a book. He sets out an introduction to the work or a 'bill of fare to the feast' so that all persons may peruse 'at their first entrance into a house'. Customers may then stay and 'regale with what is provided for them' or may seek out something better suited to their taste.

To set out the bill of fare, this book is intended for a wide range of readers and, in particular: headteachers, senior teachers and governors; school inspectors and advisers, local government officers and support staff; government employees involved in education; and educationalists in universities and colleges of higher education. It is hoped that readers from England and Wales and from other developed English-speaking countries will find the book of interest. I hope parents and others with an interest in special educational needs will also be among readers of the book.

Format of the book

The book comprises ten chapters, including a brief conclusion chapter, and an index. Each chapter has an introduction, headlined sections and a summary and conclusion. References are given at the end of each chapter.

Uses of the book

This book seeks to illustrate the importance of and encourage further developments in the use of standards of pupil achievement in the area of special educational needs (SEN). This involves considering legislation, policies, procedure and practice. The book works through various aspects of SEN to show the importance of standards of pupil achievement, the opportunities to develop further the application of pupil attainment and the challenges that sometimes arise in trying to do so.

These aspects of SEN embrace: definitions of SEN (and related terms), particularly in legislation; the assessment and identification of SEN; target setting, benchmarking and value added approaches; the issue of inclusion; and SEN funding at national and local levels. They also include the use of SEN progress and standards data in relation to pupil information (gender, ethnicity, main learning difficulty, social background and age). Other aspects of SEN covered are the use of SEN standards and progress data in relation to 'stable' school provision (quality of teaching, school organization and pupil organization) and in relation to 'variable' school provision (professional support, parents and the community). The book considers documentation including Individual Education Plans, school record keeping and school SEN policies. Finally, the role of the special school is considered.

In order to follow through the implications of this approach in a coherent way, the system considered is that in England and Wales at the time of writing. This enables a related range of topics to be considered together, including legislation, government guidance, policies, a range of approaches used in schools and possibilities for further developing the use of standards of pupil acheivement in this context.

It is hoped, however, that readers in other English-speaking developed countries will wish to consider the implications of the ideas and approaches covered in the book and the application to their own country. These countries include Scotland, Northern Ireland, the United States of America, Canada, Australia and New Zealand.

Readers from countries other than England and Wales could follow through the approach of this book, should they wish, using their own legislative structure and their own policies and practices as necessary. Some issues, such as inclusion and the quality of teaching, are common to many countries. Further, some examples of approaches from other countries are included in the text although the main focus is England and Wales.

One of the best models in literature of drawing tactful attention to imperfections is that of Herbert Pocket in Dickens's *Great Expectations*. Arriving newly in London, Pip asks Herbert for any hints if he does things wrong. As they eat their first meal together 'with London all around', Herbert sprinkles delicately into the conversation little tips (it is not the custom to put the knife in the mouth – for fear of accidents) with such good humour that Pip finds them very easy to accept. This book cannot hope to emulate such grace but one theme is as constructively as possible to suggest shortcomings in systems of SEN which do not take sufficient cognizance of standards of pupil achievement and to indicate the advantages of making standards more of a focus.

Suggestions

I would welcome any helpful comments to improve the book so that future editions may continue to be as informative as possible. Please write to me care of the publishers.

This book is dedicated to my dearest friend Malcolm Linstead.

CHAPTER 1

Defining special educational needs and related terms

Introduction

Misunderstanding can be deliciously mischievous. United States actress Tallulah Bankhead affected not to recognize the Salvation Army soldier who approached with a tambourine for the collection. Dropping 50 dollars into the instrument, she cried, 'Don't bother to thank me. I know what a perfectly ghastly season it's been for you Spanish dancers.'

However, clarity is beneficial too. This chapter therefore considers the definition of 'special educational needs' and related terms.

Disability in the United States of America

Our focus in this chapter is the definition of special educational needs in England and Wales but it is interesting first to consider briefly the definition in the USA, which differs in some important ways. A pupil requiring special education in the USA is referred to as 'disabled', whereas in England and Wales disability is one aspect of special educational needs (SEN), although a child may be disabled and not have SEN.

In the USA, all pupils with a disability are entitled under law to an Individual Education Plan (IEP). This document offers legal protection similar to that provided by the statement of SEN in England and Wales. A document also called an IEP is used in England and Wales to supplement the requirements of a statement of SEN and for pupils with less severe and less complex SEN not requiring a statement. Also in England and Wales, many pupils receive SEN services without been required to have a statement.

In the USA, pupils in need of special education covered by federal law both:

• have a defined disability; and

- need special education because the disability has an adverse educational impact.

Categories of disability under federal law as amended in 1997 (20 *United States Code* 1402, 1997) are as follows:

- mental retardation;
- traumatic brain injury;
- hearing impairment/deafness;
- visual impairment/blindness;
- speech or language impairments;
- serious emotional disturbance;
- orthopaedic impairments;
- autism;
- specific learning disabilities;
- health impairments.

Federal law reflected in state law requires that disabled children be provided with free appropriate public education individualized to the child's needs and provided in the least restrictive environment. This involves having procedures for assessing that, to the maximum extent appropriate, students with 'disabilities' in United States terminology are educated with students who are not disabled. Special classes, separate schools or other removal of students with disabilities from the 'regular' educational environment occurs only when the nature or severity of the disability is such that education in regular classes with the use of supplementary aids and services cannot be achieved satisfactorily.

This requirement is now part of the Individuals with Disabilities Education Act (IDEA) and covers over 10 per cent of the school population, for whom federal funds meet about 7 per cent of the total cost of their education (McDonnell *et al.* 1997). It is interesting to note the difference in the percentages considered to indicate the level of special educational need in England and Wales (about 16 per cent) and in the United States of America (about 10 per cent). Part of the reason for the differences may be that the percentage in England and Wales includes pupils with more severe SEN and those with less severe SEN, while in the USA the percentage appears to include those with more severe 'learning disabilities'. Nevertheless, it is important to recognize that one is not discussing a group which is not universally easily defined, like people with blue eyes or boys and girls. The identification of the group considered to have SENs or learning disabilities involves elements of educational and political judgement.

Further legal protection is afforded by the Rehabilitation Act 1973, section 504, and the Americans with Disabilities Act, which seek to assure equal opportunities for disabled people to benefit from education programmes and activities. These laws give extra legal protection to disabled pupils within the remit of the IDEA but also cover those who are not eligible for IDEA programmes. These include pupils with mild disabilities who may need limited 'accommodations' such as extra time to finish tasks (Florian and Pullin, 2000).

Pupils with disabilities must be fully included in initiatives and educational reforms (Public Law 105–17, 1997).

Special Educational Needs in Scotland and Northern Ireland

The United Kingdom comprises four countries: England, Wales, Scotland and Northern Ireland. Although the latter two have their own legal and educational systems these are often similar to those of England and Wales. The systems in England and Wales are mainly shared and operate under the same laws.

While the focus of this book in England and Wales, much of the text applies to Scotland and Northern Ireland (and other countries). At the same time, some aspects of special education in Scotland and Northern Ireland are distinctive.

In Scotland, the Education (Scotland) Act 1981 (as amended) enacted several of the recommendations of the influential Warnock Report (DES, 1978). This included bringing in recording procedures. Parents were given a right to express a preference for a school but the education authority could refuse the request on several grounds; for example, if the child's admission would effect the education of other children. A Green Paper (a government consultative paper) on special education in Scotland (SOEID, 1998) included a range of commitments. For example, every education authority is required to prepare, publish and make available a full policy on special educational needs. Where possible pupils with SEN are included in mainstream schools, both grant-aided by central government and independent, and special classes within ordinary schools. (For an interesting comparison of approaches to SEN in Scotland and the United States of America see Lange and Riddell, 2000.)

In Northern Ireland, under the Education and Libraries (NI) Order, education and library boards must provide for children and young people with SEN up to the age of nineteen. From the 1998–9 school year, Northern Ireland had a similar government code of practice on special education to that already in place in England and Wales.

Definition of SEN in England and Wales

The term special educational needs came to be commonly employed in England following its use in the Warnock Report (DES, 1978). Before then it was more usual to refer to categories of 'handicap', which had been set out under regulations following the Education Act 1944, namely blind, partially sighted, deaf, partially deaf, delicate, diabetic, educationally subnormal, epileptic, maladjusted, physically handicapped and speech defect. In this case, the change indicates rather more than expunging an earlier term soiled by negative attitudes. Indeed, the medical profession still commonly uses the expression 'handicap'. But in education, the change to 'special educational needs' indicated that the previous 'handicapping conditions' were to be seen in relation to learning and were no longer categories carrying with them the possible connotations that development was arrested and the person's learning was fixed.

Following the Warnock Report, the Education Act 1981 replaced the previous categories of handicap with a broader definition of special educational needs. These earlier categories included 'maladjusted' for what is now referred to as behavioural, emotional and social difficulties, and 'educationally subnormal-severe' for what we would presently called 'severe learning difficulties'.

In the United States terminology differs from that currently used in England and Wales, and perhaps the area most likely to be confused is that of learning difficulties. The following are rough equivalents:

England and Wales	*United States of America*
moderate learning difficulties	mild mental retardation
severe learning difficulties	moderate to severe mental retardation
profound and multiple learning difficulties	profound mental retardation

The well known broader definition of SEN in England and Wales, carried forward into later Education Acts including the Education Act 1996, emphasizes the link with learning, stating that: 'a child has special educational needs ... if he has a learning difficulty which calls for special educational provision to be made for him' (Education Act 1996, section 312). It follows from this definition that the 'learning difficulty' has to be specified. The Act does this, stating that a child has a learning difficulty if:

a) he has a significantly greater difficulty in learning than the majority of children of his age;

b) he has a disability which either prevents or hinders him from making use of educational facilities of a kind generally provided for children of his age in schools within the area of the local education authority; or

c) he is under the age of five and is, or would be if special educational provision were not made for him, likely to fall within paragraph (a) and (b) when of, or over that age. (Section 312 (2))

Learning difficulties

Sub-section (a) of section 312(2) of the Education Act 1996 relates to learning difficulty 'significantly greater' than that of children of the same age. This is indicated in slow progress and, as a result, in low standards of achievement. An example of a learning difficulty is profound and multiple learning difficulty where the pupils' progress has been very slow and where standards of achievement are considerably below those of children who do not have such difficulties.

Disability

Sub-section 312(2)(b) of the Education Act 1996 concerns 'disability', so it is important to be clear about this term too. The Children Act 1989 states that a child is disabled if he or she is blind, deaf or dumb, suffers from mental disorder of any kind or is substantially or permanently handicapped by illness, injury, congenital deformity or other such disability as may be prescribed. The Disability Discrimination Act 1995 defines a disabled person as someone who has: 'a physical or mental impairment which has a substantial and long term adverse effect on his ability to carry out normal day-to-day activities.' Not all disabled children will have a special educational need or a learning difficulty, although many will. (DfEE, 2000).

A child who is disabled may not necessarily make slower progress and have lower standards of achievement than others of the same age. In other words, the nature of the disability is not defined by standards of achievement and progress. The difficulty is in gaining access to learning and the curriculum. If provision securely gives access, then the pupil's progress and standards can be the same as or better than other children. The point is that if the pupil does not receive help in gaining this access then her education is likely to suffer.

In discussing learning difficulties and disability, it is not implied that they are always separate. A pupil with learning difficulty such as severe learning difficulties may also experience a disability such as blindness. Nor is it always easy, as we shall see in Chapter 2, to be definitive about whether some areas of SEN are most usefully considered as a learning difficulty or a disability or as both.

For a broad overview of educational legislation in England and Wales, see Farrell *et al.* (1995). For an overview of special education legislation see Farrell (2000).

The World Health Organization constructs of health-related experiences

The World Health Organization (WHO, 2000) has produced a draft document seeking to reposition earlier concepts such as disability, impairment and handicap. The earlier classification was the International Classification of Impairments, Disability and Handicap (ICIDH), which was first published by the WHO in 1980 for trialling purposes. Although the new classification is the International Classification of Functioning, Disability and Health, the WHO proposes to use the earlier acronym of ICIDH and the classification is to be ICIDH-2. Components of ICIDH-2 may be summarized as:

- body functions and structures;
- activities;
- participation;
- contextual factors.

Each of these may be expressed in terms of:

- construct of concern;
- characteristics;
- positive aspect;
- negative aspect;
- qualifiers.

If a matrix of these parameters is made, the intersection of 'negative aspect' and the four components produces the following:

- Body functions and structures–negative aspect: *impairment*.
- Activities–negative aspect: *activity limitation*.
- Participation–negative aspect: *participation restriction*.
- Contextual factors–negative aspect: *barriers/hindrances*.

The term *impairment* is understood as 'problems in body function and structure as a significant deviation or loss' (ICIDH-2, p. 11). *Activity limitation* is similar to the term 'disabilities' as used in the earlier ICIDH of 1980. *Participation restriction* is defined as 'problems an individual has in execution of task or involvement in life situations in current environment' (ICIDH-2, p. 14) and this concept is similar to the earlier notion of handicap. *Barriers/hindrances* refer to an interaction of personal and environmental factors having a negative effect on performance. It can be seen that these constructs of health-related experiences are intended to replace terms used earlier, such as 'disability' and 'handicap'.

Establishing 'needs'

When one is considering special educational needs, the word 'need' itself can be misleading, for it is linked to value judgements that may not at first be apparent. It is different to 'wants' in that needs imply a particular objective. If he is to paint, a child needs a paintbrush. If he wants a paintbrush, he may or may not wish to paint. As need implies values, it is not always possible to agree that a particular need should be satisfied. Further, to assess need, it is necessary to assess what is required for a particular end. Young children especially are unlikely to be able to judge their needs for themselves, particularly their long-term needs. Adults also differ in what they judge to be the child's needs depending on such factors as their perspective on child psychology, their sociological knowledge, their opinions of what desirable objectives are and their knowledge of means to ends. So how does this apply to special educational needs?

Wrapped up in the term special educational needs is the assumption that the child has a need that requires satisfying or should be met. The value judgements in this include that education is in itself worthwhile and that to learn is a human need. The objective is that the learner is educated as well as is possible. What is required for that particular end may be access to a building, access to a curriculum, involvement in particular approaches to teaching and learning and so on.

While such judgements seem easy to justify, it is worth remembering that in England, as recently as the 1960s, legislation considered children with severe learning difficulties as 'ineducable'. With the passing of the Education (Handicapped Children) Act 1970, implemented in 1971, local education authorities assumed from health authorities the responsibility of 'severely mentally handicapped' children and for the first time under law all children were considered to be capable of being educated.

Should context or criteria determine SEN?

SEN is defined and identified in order to determine which pupils will receive special provision over others. This preferential provision is justified by the particular circumstances of the pupil (his or her 'need'). The provision is normally that of closer individual monitoring of progress through such means as Individual Education Plans and closer attention to provision through individualized approaches or the provision of special individual equipment. If it were possible to provide these individualized approaches to provision and monitoring to all pupils there would be no point in identifying a group of pupils to be considered as those with SENs in the first place.

It follows from this that educators and others have to decide who falls into the group and who does not, although there will inevitably be some debate about pupils on the fringes of the definition of SEN and some discussion about interpretation.

In Britain in the late 1970s a committee was set up to:

> review educational provision in England, Scotland and Wales for children and young people handicapped by disabilities of body or mind taking into account the medical aspects of their needs, together with arrangements to prepare them for entry into employment; to consider the most effective use of resources for these purposes.

The subsequent influential report, known as the Warnock Report (DES, 1978), maintained that the term special education should be broadened. Before then the preferred concept was 'categories of handicap'. The committee considered among many other issues what would be a reasonable proportion of pupils to consider as having SEN. Their formulation was that about one child in six or just below 17 per cent at any one time will need some form of special education.

Around one child in five or about 20 per cent of children at some time in their school career will need some form of special education. These figures have often been incorrectly remembered by educationalists in Britain to suggest that around 20 per cent of children at any one time would need some form of special education. But the main point is that an attempt was made to give a reasonable proportion of pupils that it would be appropriate to consider as having SENs.

The consideration of such a percentage is useful if the population concerned is very large, such as that of Britain or that of a large region. In that context, it is meaningful to speak of about 17 per cent of pupils 'having' SEN. However, if the population is small, such as that of a school, it is less likely that a percentage will invariably be a useful indicator of SEN.

This may be illustrated by taking an example of a sub-group of pupils within those considered as having SEN. Take the example of blindness. If it was accepted in a country that blind pupils received special educational provision (being taught Braille, mobility training and so on), then it would make sense to speak of this proportion of pupils receiving special education and having SEN. This might apply to around one pupil in a thousand. It would be accepted that not every school with a thousand pupils would necessarily have a blind pupil. Some such schools might have none, while others might have several.

It would be strange if one of the schools with no blind pupils claimed to have a blind pupil or several blind pupils (let us say because funds were allocated for providing for blind pupils) simply because statistically it could have had a blind pupil. The determining criterion would be that blindness would be clearly defined and if a school patently had no such pupils then any protestations that it did or any claim for funding would be dismissed. Objective criteria would save the system from being abused.

When other aspects of SEN are considered, the same principles may be applied. Take the example of a specific learning difficulty mainly manifesting itself as a difficulty with reading. If it was accepted in a country that pupils with reading difficulties received special educational provision (individualized reading programmes, laptop computers and so on), then it would make sense to speak of this proportion of pupils receiving special education and having SEN. It might be around ten pupils in a hundred. It would be accepted that not every school with a hundred pupils would necessarily have ten pupils with reading difficulties. Some such schools might have less while others might have many more.

It would be strange if one of the schools with few pupils with reading difficulties claimed to have 10 per cent (let us say because funds were allocated for providing for pupils with reading difficulties) simply because statistically it could have had ten per cent of such pupils. The determining criterion would be to establish a level of reading difficulty indicated by attainment in reading. If the school clearly had only a few pupils with reading difficulties then any protestations that it had more or any claim for funding inflated numbers would be dismissed. Objective criteria would again save the system from being abused.

The school with few pupils with reading difficulties might claim that the proportion of pupils that it had been agreed was taken to exist nationally ought to apply to it. It might argue that, although its pupils did not have the level of reading difficulties as severe as any criteria would require, it did have pupils who were behind other pupils in the school. Therefore, in the context of the school it had pupils who had learning difficulties greater than their peers.

On this contextual approach a selective school for very able pupils could claim that 49 per cent of its pupils had SEN relating to reading difficulties because they were behind (statistically) the majority of the pupils in the school. Particularly where the fair allocation of funding is involved this would lead to funds being allocated to where they were least needed rather than to where they are most needed.

Criteria, then, should determine SEN rather than the vagaries of individual school context. These criteria are often in turn related to standards of pupil achievement, or they may be based on measurable criteria such as hearing loss in the case of the disability of hearing impairment.

Manageability

To define SEN according to criteria including that of standards is to raise the issue of manageability. It may be decided that a certain percentage of pupils (say 17 per cent) are to be deemed to have SEN at any one time and to receive special provision mainly in the form of individualized approaches and individual monitoring. We have already mentioned that this level of educational difficulty is not necessarily evenly spread across individual schools.

The situation is manageable where a small percentage of pupils have SEN in any one school. It is more difficult where a school, according to agreed criteria, has many more than 17 per cent of its pupils with SEN, who by definition would benefit from individual provision and individualized monitoring. A point is reached where the school can no longer keep track of the individualized planning, provision and monitoring, and chasing and maintaining paperwork begins to take precedence over the education of the pupils.

One practicable approach here is to concentrate on a manageable percentage of pupils with the greatest learning difficulties and to seek to provide for the other pupils through whole-school strategies, including multiprofessional approaches. This could be achieved if equitable funding was allocated to the school according to the number of pupils it has with SEN.

Standards (broadly defined) and progress

Standards is a general expression with a wide application. In the theatre, critics, as the judges of standards and arbiters of taste, can be searing. Heywood Brown said of one production he witnessed, 'It opened at 8.40 sharp and closed at 10.40 dull.' Dorothy Parker famously said of Katherine Hepburn's performance in a Broadway show, 'She ran the whole gamut of emotions from A to B.'

Educational standards are considered quite broadly in the model implicit in the framework used in England and Wales by school inspectors (OFSTED, 1999a,b,c). The evaluation schedule for inspection is seen in terms of: context and overview; outcomes; quality of provision; efficiency and effectiveness of management; and issues for the school. The area relating to standards is that of 'outcomes'. Outcomes are interpreted as standards relating to: the school's results and pupils' achievements; pupils' attitudes, values and personal development; and attendance.

The standards with which we are concerned are also quite broad and relate to pupil achievement. They include standards relating to English and mathematics and to other curriculum subjects. In some instances of SEN they also concern standards relating to the particular main learning difficulty of a pupil, such as the standard of speech and language when a pupil is compared with others of the same age.

Judgements on standards and progress are factors helping to determine whether some pupils have learning difficulties. In other words, the judgement that a child's level of learning difficulty is greater than that of others of the same age is made according to the standard of achievement of the child and the rate of progress that he or she makes.

The inclusion of personal and social development as an aspect of standards is important. This is not to say that standards of academic attainment are not equally valued. Indeed, self-esteem, as an aspect of personal and social development, is likely to be enhanced if a pupil reaches higher standards of academic attainment. However, the importance of personal and social development is hard to overestimate.

Where the SEN are related to disability, standards of achievement do not help to define SEN in the same way that they do for, say, moderate learning difficulties. However, the disability implies an obstacle to access to learning and the curriculum. The success with which any SEN provision aids access will be reflected in the educational progress made by the pupil and the standards of achievement reached. Consequently, standards are central in being the basis of the definition of learning difficulties and an indication of the success of provision for both learning difficulties and disabilities.

'Prior attainment' in relation to standards

Ability may be maligned, as when Ambrose Bierce in his *Devil's Dictionary* defines a connoisseur as a specialist who knows everything about something and nothing about anything else. But it is also in education a problematic concept.

When making judgements about the progress of pupils with SEN in lesson observations and elsewhere, Office for Standards in Education (OFSTED) school inspectors used to express their judgements in terms of pupils of lower ability (judgements were also made about pupils of middle ability and higher ability). It is now more common for judgements to be related to 'prior attainment'. This is presumably because it is so difficult to judge the ability of a pupil, as it has implications of potential as well as performance. Such potential is difficult enough for a teacher to make when he knows the pupil well. It is almost impossible for an outside person such as an inspector to come to a secure judgement on this when she sees the pupil only for a short time.

Low prior attainment, if associated with slow progress, is likely to lead to low standards of current attainment. The combination of low prior attainment and slow progress leading to low present attainment can therefore be seen as part of the definition of learning difficulties.

As has already been indicated, when we discuss learning difficulties and disability, it is not implied that they are necessarily separate. The main point of the discussion here is that standards are important in the definition of many areas of SEN and an indicator that provision is effective in all areas of SEN.

A particular aspect of prior attainment is baseline assessment and this is considered as an indicator of value added in Chapter 3, on 'Curriculum and assessment and target setting'.

Potential confusion between SEN and other factors
Pupils who have English as an additional language

In *Bleak House*, Dickens uses the metaphor of fog creeping around Chancery to indicate the labyrinthine and confusing paths of the law. An equally confusing blanket of fog hovers around the issue of SEN and pupils for whom English is an additional language unless one is precise.

Children for whom English is an additional language may be incorrectly considered as having learning difficulties. This would happen simply because they may be attaining at a lower level, say in literacy, than other children because of the limited time which they have been learning English. If such a child has low attainment in English but learns at a satisfactory rate or better, it is of course incorrect to consider the child to have special educational needs as defined in the Education Act 1996.

Learning difficulty, then, can be understood in relation to low standards and slow progress in the same way that high ability can be understood in relation to high standards and rapid progress. Indeed, the slow progress may lead to the low attainment just as the rapid progress may lead to high attainment.

Pupils with low attainment because of poor opportunities

In a similar way, caution is urged on teachers in making too early judgements that very young children (for example, through baseline assessment) may have learning difficulties because of low attainment. Such low attainment may, for example, reflect poor educational opportunities at home. The child may at school make progress in learning that indicates that he or she does not have learning difficulties.

It may be that the poor opportunities that a child has experienced before entering school have not only appeared to lead to low attainment but also contributed to slow progress. The child's capacity to learn, to use thinking skills, and to explore may have been inhibited or discouraged so that the two concomitants of learning difficulties, low attainment and slow progress, are apparent. In this case it is appropriate that the child be considered as having SEN. The main point is that it cannot always be assumed that because a child enters a school attaining at a lower level than other children, he or she does not have the capacity to progress rapidly and catch up. This is of course a subtle and important educational judgement for teachers and others to make.

Very able pupils

Sometimes, teachers and others speak of pupils who are very able as having SEN, and this can be confusing. If pupils with learning difficulties can be defined in relation to low standards and slow progress, then the very able pupil can be defined as attaining high standards and making fast progress. Therefore a pupil who is very able would not by definition have learning difficulties by virtue of her high ability. It is better to refer to very able pupils as having particular needs rather than SEN. Neither would it be reasonable to view very able pupils as by definition having a disability which hindered them from making use of the normal education facilities.

Of course a pupil may be very able in one aspect of attainment, such as physical education, and have learning difficulties in another area of learning, such as English, perhaps because of a specific learning difficulty. A pupil may be very able in some school subjects but may have emotional and behavioural difficulties constituting a SEN. Further, occasionally pupils with severe learning difficulties may have an area of average or better than average skill or knowledge, such as a memory for dates, musical skill or skill in drawing.

SUMMARY

The definition of SEN in England and Wales in the Education Act 1996 was considered. Learning difficulty and disability were discussed. Standards were defined broadly to include not only academic standards but also personal and social development and the standards reached in these areas. 'Prior attainment' was considered in relation to progress and current standards of attainment.

Potential confusion between SEN and other factors was considered with reference to pupils for whom English is an additional language, pupils with low attainment because of poor opportunities and very able pupils.

Standards of pupil achievement are important in the definition of many areas of SEN and an indicator that provision is effective in all areas of SEN.

References

DES (1978) *Special Educational Needs: Report of the Committee of Enquiry into the Education of Handicapped Children and Young People* (The Warnock Report). London: HMSO.

DfE (1994) *The Code of Practice on the Identification and Assessment of Special Educational Needs.* London: Department for Education.

DfEE (2000) *SEN and Disability Rights in Education Bill: Consultation Document.* London, Edinburgh and Cardiff: Department for Education and Employment, Scottish Executive, Scotland Office and Cynulliad Cenedlaethol Cymru.

Farrell, M. (1998) 'New Terms for Old'. *The SLD Experience,* **21** Summer, 16–17.

Farrell, M. (2000) *The Special Education Handbook,* 2nd edn. London: David Fulton.

Farrell, M., Kerry, T. and Kerry, C. (1995) *The Blackwell Handbook of Education.* Oxford: Blackwell.

Florian, L. and Pullin, D. (2000) 'Defining difference: a comparative perspective on legal and policy issues in educational reform and special educational needs' in M. J. McLaughlin and M. Rouse (eds) *Special Education and School Reform in the United States and Great Britain.* London: Routledge.

Lange, C. and Riddell, S. (2000) 'Special educational needs policy and choice: tensions between policy development in the US and UK contexts', in M. J. McLaughlin and M. Rouse (eds) *Special Education and School Reform in the United States and Great Britain.* London: Routledge.

McDonnell, L., McLaughlin, M. and Morison, P. (eds) (1997) *Educating One and All: Students with Disabilities and Standards Based Reform.* Washington, D.C: National Academy Press.

OFSTED (1999a) *Handbook for Inspecting Primary Schools with Guidance on Self-evaluation.* London: The Stationery Office.

OFSTED (1999b) *Handbook for Inspecting Secondary Schools with Guidance on Self-evaluation.* London: The Stationery Office.

OFSTED (1999c) *Handbook for Inspecting Special Schools and Pupil Referral Units with Guidance on Self-evaluation.* London: The Stationery Office.

SOIED (1998) *Achievement for All.* Edinburgh: Scottish Office Education and Industry Department.

WHO (2000) *International Classification of Functioning, Disability and Health* (ICIDH-2 Pre-final Draft). Madrid: World Health Organization.

CHAPTER 2

Identifying, assessing and providing for SEN

Introduction

A child at a matinee performance of a review innocently combined identification and assessment in a devastating way when he was heard to say of Hermione Gingold in a loud whisper, 'Mummy, what is that lady *for*?' If anyone had asked in the year 2000 what the government's *SEN Code of Practice* (DfEE, 2000a) was for, the answer was straightforward. It was to try to bring further clarity to a potentially opaque area.

The SEN Code of Practice

The *SEN Code of Practice* gives practical guidance to various parties on their responsibilities towards all children with SEN. These groups include local education authorities (LEAs) and the governing bodies of all maintained schools; that is, schools for which the LEA has financial and administrative responsibility. It is permeated with references to standards and access both implicitly and explicitly. Each of its ten chapters will be considered to explore and illustrate these themes.

Principles and policies

Chapter 1 concerns 'principles and policies'. It explains (para. 1.1) that the purpose of the Code is to provide practical guidance to various parties on the discharge of their functions under part 4 of the Education Act 1996. The parties concerned are:

- local education authorities;
- the governing bodies of all maintained schools and providers of government-funded early education and those who help them (including health services and social services).

The Code sets out guidance on policies and procedures seeking to enable pupils with SEN to:

- reach their full potential;
- be fully included in their school communities;
- make a successful transition to adulthood.

One of the fundamental principles of the Code is that children with SEN should have their needs met while a critical success factor is that the 'culture, practice, management and development of resources in school or setting should be designed to ensure that all children's needs are met'.

The Code (1.5) advises that strategies be adopted which recognize different 'levels and complexities of need' and the associated range of variation in provision which reflects and promotes 'common recognition' of the continuum of SEN.

Partnership

Chapter 2 of the Code concerns 'working in partnership with parents' and Chapter 3 relates to 'pupil participation'. The chapter relating to parents speaks of children's 'needs' without reference to standards. The chapter on pupil participation briefly (3.4) alludes to 'achievements' being noted as part of the process of Individual Educational Plans and of pupils being encouraged to track their own progress and record achievement. Chapter 10 deals with 'working in partnership with other agencies'.

Identification, assessment and provision

Chapters 4 to 6 concern respectively identification, assessment and provision in:

- early education settings (Chapter 4);
- the primary phase (Chapter 5);
- the secondary sector (Chapter 6).

Chapter 4, concerning early education settings, identifies providers which are eligible for government funding as including:

- maintained mainstream and special schools (maintained schools being schools for which the LEA has financial and administrative responsibility);
- maintained nursery schools;
- independent schools;
- non-maintained special schools;
- local authority day care providers (e.g. day nurseries, family centres);

- other registered day care providers (e.g. pre-schools, play groups, private day nurseries);
- local authority portage schemes;
- accredited child minders working as part of an approved network.

The government's Early Learning Goals set out what most children will achieve in various 'areas' (such as communication, language and literacy, and mathematical development) by the time they enter year 1 of primary education. Early education concerns children aged three to five years and is known as the 'foundation stage' of education. The identification of SEN is related to slow progress in the foundation stage. The provider intervenes through Early Years Action and, if progress is still not satisfactory, the SEN coordinator may seek advice and support from external agencies (Early Years Action Plus) (4.3).

Various triggers are proposed for intervention through Early Years Action (4.7). These concern lack of progress or insufficient progress despite intervention in the areas of emotional and/or behavioural difficulties and sensory or physical problems. They also concern communication and/or interaction difficulties which require 'specific individual interventions' to access learning. As well as rates of progress and access, another trigger is standards; that is, a child who continues working at levels 'significantly below those expected for children of a similar age in certain areas' (4.7).

Triggers are also indicated for outside intervention through Early Years Action Plus. These also concern standards, progress and access. One (standards) trigger is that the child 'continues working at an early years curriculum substantially below that expected of children of a similar age'. Another (progress) trigger is that the child 'continues to make little or no progress in specific areas over a long period'. A further (implicit) progress trigger is that the child has sensory or physical needs which 'require' additional equipment or regular visits for direct intervention or advice from practitioners from a specialist service. The reasons for the 'requirement' are not spelled out but are presumably because the child has not made satisfactory progress. An access trigger is that the child has continuing communication or interaction difficulties which 'impede the development of social relationships and cause substantial barriers to learning'. The implication is that the 'barriers' are those in the way of access to learning and access to the curriculum.

Chapter 5 of the Code concerns identification, assessment and provision in the primary phase (five to eleven years) or National Curriculum years 1 to 6. Triggers for School Action, like those relating to early years settings, concern progress and attainment despite the child receiving differentiated learning opportunities. One progress trigger, for example (5.12), concerns sensory or physical problems, and the child 'continues to make little or no progress despite the provision of specialist equipment'. An attainment trigger is that the child 'shows signs of difficulty in developing literacy or numeracy skills which result in poor attainment in some curriculum areas'. Another trigger which implies unsatisfactory progress and perhaps relates to access to learning is that the child 'presents persistent emotional or behavioural difficulties which are not ameliorated by the behaviour management techniques usually employed in the school' (5.12).

Triggers for School Action Plus (5.16) again involve standards, progress and access. Each trigger assumes that the child has already been receiving an individualized programme and/or concentrated support under School Action. One (progress) trigger is that the child still 'continues to make little or no progress in specific areas over a long period'. Another (standards) trigger is that the child 'continues working at National Curriculum levels substantially below that expected of children of a similar age'. A target relating to progress and access is that the child 'has ongoing communication or interaction difficulties that impede the development of social relationships and cause substantial barriers to learning'.

Chapter 6 deals with 'identification, assessment and provision in the secondary sector'. Triggers for School Action involve progress, attainment and (possibly) access. They all assume that the pupil has received differentiated learning opportunities (6.12). A progress trigger is that the pupil has 'sensory or physical problems and continues to make little or no progress despite the provision of specialist equipment'. An attainment trigger is that the pupil 'shows signs of difficulty in developing literacy or numeracy skills that result in poor attainment in some curriculum areas'. A trigger that appears to include progress and access is that a pupil 'presents persistent emotional and/or behavioural difficulties which are not ameliorated by the behaviour management techniques usually employed in the school'.

School Action Plus triggers (6.16) again concern standards, attainment and access. It is assumed that pupils are receiving an individual programme and/or concentrated support. A progress trigger is that the pupil 'continues to have difficulty in developing literacy and numeracy skills'. An attainment trigger is that the pupil 'continues working at National Curriculum levels substantially below that expected of pupils of a similar age'. A trigger relating to access to learning (of both pupils with SEN and other) is that the pupil 'has emotional or behavioural difficulties which substantially and regularly interfere with their own learning or that of the class group, despite having an individualized behaviour management programme'.

Statutory assessments, statements and annual reviews

Chapters 7, 8 and 9 of the Code refer respectively to 'statutory assessment of SEN', 'statement of SEN' and 'annual review'.

The statutory assessment of SEN has to do with the duties of a local education authority under the Education Act 1996 sections 321 and 323. This is to identify and make a statutory assessment of those children for whom they are responsible who have SEN and who probably need a statement. If a school requests a statutory assessment on a child, among the evidence that it must provide is evidence of the pupil's rate of progress, or lack of progress, over time (7.4).

One aspect of considering whether a statutory assessment is necessary is that an LEA will always wish to see evidence of a child's level of academic attainment and rate of progress (7.10). Evidence of attainment is considered in section 7.12, which points out that key indicators are the results of assessments and tests in the core subjects of the National Curriculum (at the end of key stages) and the outcomes of baseline assessment. An individual child's attainments 'must always be understood in the context of the attainment of the child's peers'. It is interesting that the term 'peers' is used rather than (as in the legal definition) 'children of the same age' (Education Act 1996 section 312). This is presumably because 'peers' refers to other pupils in the same class or group. So what does it mean? This contextual remark does not presumably mean that the child should be considered to have SEN if he is attaining at or about expected National Curriculum levels but his school peers are attaining better.

If this were so, it would have implications for local funding (for example, by LEAs). Consider two sets of evidence. The first relates to a pupil who is behind nationally expected National Curriculum levels in one school where peers are similarly behind. The second evidence relates to a pupil who is attaining at or above expected National Curriculum levels but whose peers are attaining at higher levels still. If the contextual peers approach were taken, evidence relating to the first pupil might not carry the same weight as that relating to the second pupil. In other words, if school (peer) context was a key determinant for deciding on statutory assessment of SEN then pupils could acquire statements at very different levels of attainment. This would seem to go against the principle of giving greater support to those with the greatest learning difficulty (in more absolute terms).

Another possible interpretation of the term 'peers' is indicated in section 7.12 of the Code which states: 'A child's apparently weak performance may, on examination of the evidence, be attributable to wider factors associated with the school's organisation.' This implies that, although a child may be achieving at low levels, her 'performance' may relate to aspects of school organization. The assumption is that, should the aspect of school organization relating to the pupil's performance be modified, her performance will improve. The Code goes on to state: 'Careful consideration of evidence of low attainment may reveal good progress from a low base' (7.12). This would imply that 'weak performance', as indicated in low attainment, may not necessarily be an indicator of SEN because the school organization (or some other school factor) is inhibiting learning. Once this is adjusted, then performance would be expected to improve and progress be such that it may not indicate SEN.

Another way in which this could arise is with a pupil for whom English is an additional language but who does not have SEN. Low attainment for such a pupil in, for instance, English would be likely to reflect lack of familiarity with the language and rapid progress would indicate that the pupil did not have SEN in that area.

Similar potential confusion arises when the Code advises LEAs to be alert to various 'discrepancies'. These include a discrepancy between:

1. A child's attainment in assessments and tests in core subjects of the National Curriculum.
2. The performance expected of the child as indicated by a consensus among those who have taught and observed the child, including his or her parents, and supported by such standardized tests as can reliably be administered (7.12).

One interpretation of this is that the LEA should be alerted if a test of intelligence indicates a very high quotient and the attainment of a child, in say, mathematics was at levels expected of pupils of the same age nationally. It could be argued that the discrepancy between the very high IQ score and merely average mathematics attainment should 'alert' the LEA to the possibility that the child may have SEN. Returning to the parity argument outlined earlier in this chapter, the discrepancy approach could go against the principle of greater resources being allocated according to greater levels of learning difficulty as indicated by the slowest progress and the lowest attainment.

This parity argument carries more weight in an LEA structure than in the independent sector. In the LEA or state setting a limited amount of funds is being allocated in a way which it is hoped is equitable. Low attainment and slow progress along with significantly blocked access to learning and the curriculum are ways of helping to determine the 'need' and therefore the appropriate support and funding.

In the independent sector, parents may choose to pay extra to have their child provided with a more individualized approach (and identified as having SEN as a precursor to this, perhaps). Parity is less important in such cases. Consider that as a whole a selective independent school performs well above the national average and a pupil in it performs only at the level of the national average. It may be acceptable to the child's parents to have the child identified as having SEN and for them to pay more for more individualized approaches to assessment and/or provision.

Again the Code appears to return to the more 'absolute' view of attainment as it applies to SEN by stating that the LEA should 'therefore seek clear recorded evidence of the child's academic attainment'. The LEA should ask whether

> there is evidence that the child is falling progressively behind the majority of children of his or her age in academic attainment in any of the National Curriculum core subjects, as measured by standardised tests and the teacher's own recorded assessments of the child's classroom work, including any portfolios of the child's work. (7.12)

Broad areas of SEN are identified, given that they are not rigid and that there may be a considerable degree of overlap between them. These areas are:

- communication and interaction;
- cognition and learning;
- behaviour, emotional and social development;
- sensory or physical.

Chapter 8, 'Statement of SEN', outlines the procedures for making statements and the time scales involved. Chapter 9 covers the 'annual review' of the statement of SEN and the necessary procedures involved.

Thresholds

A further document related to the Code provides guidance (DfEE, 2000b). It was derived from research by the Special Needs Research Centre at the University of Newcastle upon Tyne, England. The document indicates thresholds for School Action and School Action Plus in four areas:

- communication and interaction;
- cognition and learning;
- behaviour, emotional and social development;
- sensory and physical.

Cognition and learning are considered in terms of general and specific learning difficulties. Lower and higher levels of general learning difficulty are indicated according to performance and attainment. For example, higher levels of difficulty may be shown by (among other indicators) performance within the National Curriculum 'outside the range within which most children are expected to work (i.e. level W at the end of KS 1, level 1 at KS2, level 2 at KS3)' (4.1); (level W means 'working towards' level 1 of the national curriculum). There are also indicators of progress. Specific learning difficulty thresholds also include reference to 'performance'. For example, higher levels of difficulty may be indicated by 'literacy performance in the first or second centile as measured by standardised tests which makes it very difficult for pupils to access written materials or perform writing tasks in any area of the curriculum' (4.5).

Behavioural, emotional and social difficulties are considered at lower and higher levels of difficulty. In a general description, age-inappropriate behaviour is given as an indication. Standards apply only in a broad sense to behavioural, emotional and social difficulties. If one accepts that age-appropriate development has not taken place or has been thrown off course, then one can regard pupils with difficulties in this area as not having developed or learned behaviour, emotional responses and social skills at a level that most others of the same age have. However, in some cases, it is clear that it is not that 'standards' of development have not been reached, but that unbearable life experiences such as emotional or physical abuse have shattered personal ability. Even in such instances, special educational needs can be addressed not only by drawing on psychotherapeutic approaches, but also by taking an educational view of shaping behaviour and social skills to help a child to manage his or her difficult behaviour.

Communication and interaction difficulties are considered in relation to speech and language difficulties and to autistic spectrum disorders. Difficulties are understood in terms of (among other features) attainment. For instance, lower levels of difficulties may show themselves as 'measurable speech and language skills which are somewhat below those of the majority of peers' (6.1). Higher levels of difficulty may be understood in terms of progress as well as other features, and an indicator is 'low rates of progress in many areas of the curriculum ... and particularly in literacy' (6.1). Autistic spectrum disorders do not lend themselves particularly well to a standards and progress perspective and only a little better to an access view. This is because autism is a syndrome leading to life-long and severe impairment characterized by severe difficulties in communication, social development and imagination.

Sensory and physical difficulties are considered as hearing impairment, visual impairment and physical and medical difficulties. In the case of hearing impairment, lower levels are indicated by 'progress in the curriculum, but at lower levels than might be expected from performance on tasks where hearing ability is not central and/or from measures of cognitive skills' (7.1). At higher levels of hearing difficulty, an indication is 'attainment levels in tasks and curriculum areas most affected by pupils' hearing impairments falling well below what might be expected on measures of cognitive skills' (7.1).

However, a central issue is not just standards, but access to learning and the curriculum that is necessary. This may be aided in various ways, such as with specialized equipment and approaches to learning. A similar perspective may be taken of visual impairment and of physical and medical difficulties.

SUMMARY

Throughout the Code of Practice, attainment, progress and access to learning and curriculum are important features. They are important in early years settings, in the primary phase and in the secondary sector at School Action, Action Plus and statutory assessment. They are important at lower and higher levels of learning difficulties.

Standards and progress are particularly pertinent in relation to general learning difficulties, specific learning difficulties and speech and language difficulties. They may be less central to some behavioural, emotional and social difficulties, although there are ways in which a standards and progress perspective is useful.

Issues around access to learning and the curriculum are particularly important in hearing impairment, visual impairment and physical and medical difficulties. They also arise in the case of behavioural, emotional and social difficulties, where the issues are not just the access of the pupil with these difficulties but also the access of other pupils whose learning disruptive pupils may adversely affect. To some degree, access to learning and the curriculum has a bearing on autistic spectrum disorders.

To generalize, it is helpful to regard general learning difficulties, specific learning difficulties and speech and language difficulties as primarily 'learning difficulties'. Hearing impairment, visual impairment, physical and medical difficulties and to some degree behavioural, emotional and social difficulties may be regarded as primarily 'disabilities'. In this perspective, 'learning difficulties' are defined according to standards and progress, and the effectiveness of provision may be judged according to how it increases progress and raises standards. 'Disability' may be seen in terms of access to learning and the curriculum. The severity of the disability is judged according to the extent to which it hinders access to learning and the curriculum. The effectiveness of provision is judged according to the extent to which it aids access.

However, there is an important sense related to disability in which standards of achievement permeate special education. A disabled pupil may require access to learning and the curriculum. The degree to which this access is successfully provided will influence the educational standards the pupil achieves and the progress he or she makes. In this respect the concept of standards is still key.

This is not to say that 'learning difficulties' do not involve issues of access to the curriculum or that 'disabilities' are divorced from issues relating to standards and progress. However, the generalization appears to reflect a potentially helpful area of focus. While standards and progress may be taken to indicate the existence and severity of 'learning difficulties', the nature of disabilities is that at a certain level of severity, it is not considered necessary to have recourse to standards and progress to justify provision and funding. One does not wait for a blind child to fall behind in reading before providing for the impairment.

References

DfEE (2000a) *SEN Code of Practice on the Assessment of Pupils with Special Educational Needs*. London: Department for Education and Employment.

DfEE (2000b) *SEN Thresholds: Good Practice Guidance on Identification and Provision for Pupils with Special Educational Needs* (Consultation Document). London: Department for Education and Employment.

CHAPTER 3

Curriculum and assessment and target-setting

Introduction

'Anything that is worth doing,' declared the writer Max Beerbohm, 'has been done frequently. Things hitherto undone should be given, I suspect, a wide berth.' This view warns against too risky originality, and perhaps reminds us that however admirable originality may be, there is also merit in commonality.

Such a common view is at the heart of the standards view of the curriculum and assessment developing in both England and Wales and the United States of America. This is evident in the National Curriculum arrangement for England and Wales and in content and performance standards in the USA. This common framework is a factor in the use of target-setting and related issues.

Curriculum and assessment in England and Wales

In England and Wales, the Conservative government which was voted into power in 1979 introduced the Education Reform Act 1988 with a view to raising standards. The Act shifted responsibility for the content of the curriculum and its delivery and for assessment from local education authorities, schools and teachers towards central government. This involved provision for:

- a national curriculum;
- a national system of assessment and testing at ages 7, 11, 14 and 16;
- open enrolment;
- competition between schools for pupil places;
- parental preferences for schools;
- the setting up of other types of schools outside local education author-ity control (an example of such schools is a grant-maintained school,

which was a primary or secondary school financed through the Funding Agency for Schools after parents had voted that the school come out of local education authority control; another is city technology colleges, funded through the City Technology Colleges Trust);

- more financial independence for schools through such developments as local management for schools (LMS) and local management for special schools (LMSS).

School provision was seen in terms of key stages. Key Stage 1 was for pupils in year groups 1 to 2 (ages 5 to 7 years). Key Stage 2 was for years 3 to 6 (ages 7 to 11 years). Key Stage 3 was for years 7 to 9 (ages 11 to 14). Key Stage 4 was for years 10 to 11 (ages 14 to 16). National Curriculum subjects were identified as English, mathematics and science (the core subjects) and the 'foundation' subjects of technology, geography, history, physical education, art, music and (for Key Stage 3) a modern foreign language.

Programmes of study set out what should be taught and the expected standards of pupil attainment were set out in 'attainment targets'. In 1995, the National Curriculum was reviewed and 'level descriptions' were introduced for subjects. Instead of 'level descriptions' for art, music and physical education, 'key stage descriptions' were used. These allowed teachers to give indications of pupil levels of achievement. At the end of each key stage, summative assessments are made involving teacher assessment and 'external' tests and tasks (also known as Standards Assessment Tasks or SATs).

At the end of Key Stage 4, pupil achievement is predominantly assessed through pupil examinations such as the General Certificate of Secondary Education (GCSE) and the General National Vocational Qualifications (GNVQs) in various subjects.

The review of the National Curriculum led to various changes, including the provision of 'access statements' in each subject order. These encourage:

- the use of aids;
- adaptations to equipment;
- adaptations to communication;
- work on curriculum content to help to ensure its relevance to pupils with SEN;
- a more important place for personal and social education.

In a further revision of the national curriculum in 2000, more changes were made, including greater attention to personal and social education and a statement of inclusion. The inclusion statement sets out three principles for developing a more inclusive curriculum:

1. Setting suitable learning challenges.
2. Responding to pupils' diverse learning needs.
3. Overcoming potential barriers to learning and assessment for individuals and groups of pupils (DfEE, 1999a, p. 30, 1999b, p. 32).

Curriculum and assessment in the USA

In the United States of America, developments have occurred with some similarities to those in England and Wales. New content and performance standards have been developed to help to provide an area of common content and standards and more accountability so that all pupils have the chance to learn academically challenging subject material. It is envisaged that this will also give greater equity across schools and districts (McLaughlin and Tilstone, 2000).

Key legislation is Public Law (PL) 103–227. This federal legislation, the Goals 2000: Educate America Act, enacted in 1994, set out national education goals intended to be achieved by the year 2000. It encouraged the adoption of state standards and state assessments and increased state-level accountability for pupil achievement. At the same time, schools and local districts were to be given more discretion in their use of federal targeted resources.

A further important law is the Improving America's Schools Act (IASA), which is PL 103–328: Title 1, enacted in 1994. This introduced new conditions for acquiring funds under a federal school aid programme relating to poor, under-achieving pupils. States have to provide plans to receive Title 1 grants which provide for:

• challenging content and performance standards;
• state assessments;
• annual reports on meeting standards;
• provision for teacher support and learning in line with the new curriculum standards and assessments;
• assessment results to be disaggregated by disability, race, gender, English proficiency, migrant status and economic status (McLaughlin and Tilstone, 2000).

The Individual with Disabilities Education Act (IDEA) is federal legislation concerning the framework for special education policy. Within this framework, attempts have been made to improve pupil outcomes through the greater inclusion of disabled pupils in mainstream classrooms and through improving access to the general education curriculum and assessments.

Recent requirements aim to bring the IDEA framework into line with the approach to school improvement (in PL 103–227) and other legislation.

These requirements include that the state must establish goals for the performance of children and young people with disabilities and develop ways of determining progress on the goals. States must gather data on pupil progress, including graduation rates. Regarding assessments, children with disabilities must normally be included in general education state and district assessments. For those with disabilities who cannot take part, state and district authorities must carry out alternative assessments and report these. Changes to Individual Education Plan requirements reflect an intention that special educational provision will become more part of general education policies and classroom approaches.

Considerable variation is to be found in state approaches to content standards; for example, in the degree of detail to which the standards are expressed. There was variation in the extent to which individual states made content standards more inclusive and accessible to those with disabilities (Goertz and Friedman, 1996). More recent legislation (reauthorizing IDEA) is likely to lead to less variation.

Issues for SEN

Samuel Johnson considered that 'All knowledge is of itself of some value. There is nothing so minute or inconsiderable, that I would not rather know it than not.' From the point of view of special educational needs, a standards approach to the curriculum and to assessment can provide very useful knowledge.

Among the strengths of the approach is that it gives a structure in which national and local standards can be known. It also provides a framework against which the inclusion of pupils with SEN into general education and assessment can be judged (and the degree to which alternative curricula and assessment are necessary).

The challenges of the approach include the need for care and skill in making the agreed curriculum accessible to pupils with SEN or deciding to adapt the curriculum. Where access is particularly difficult, the curriculum may have to be modified so that the lower levels are reachable by pupils with the most severe SEN and so that the steps between the various levels of the curriculum are made smaller as appropriate to these pupils. Different pedagogical approaches may be necessary for pupils with SEN, such as devoting more time than usual to certain areas of the curriculum, some frequent and discrete teaching of functional skills, more individual teaching and physical aids and prompts.

In the assessment of pupils with SEN the general national structure may not be suitable or sufficient on its own. The collating of information to provide a broad indication of standards (for example, the test and task levels related to the National Curriculum in England and Wales) may not discern gains in learning which are small or not spread across a wide area of learning. More detailed approaches to assessment should complement broader assessment level judgements. Further, ways of making assessment accessible are necessary. These include more time, an amanuensis and physical aids (e.g. visual aids).

Where accommodations are made, however, they may be so extensive that they can no longer be regarded as a standards form of assessment. In such cases it is necessary to develop alternative forms of assessment which are agreed and as far as possible made similar. One example of this in England and Wales is the 'p' scale (e.g. DfEE, 1998). These scales seek to describe levels of achievement in the areas of language and literacy, mathematics, and personal and social development for pupils working at a level below level 1 of the national curriculum. An example of an item on this framework is level 'p1' for mathematics–number: 'pupils are beginning to show sensory awareness in relation to a range of people, objects and materials in everyday contexts. They show reflex responses to sensory stimuli, e.g. startle response.' Another example is the 'Equals' curriculum and related assessment. Equals is an organization of schools for pupils with severe learning difficulties and profound and multiple learning difficulties.

Carrying out tests under controlled conditions may also prove difficult. This is because of a tension between creating controlled conditions (which help to ensure that the results can be fairly compared with those of others) and being flexible enough to gain an accurate picture of the pupil's attainment level (Rouse and Agbenu, 1998).

A useful summary of scenarios for assessment and examples of accommodations is envisaged under the IDEA (s.612) enacted in the United States of America (Rouse et al., 2000). These can be generalized to other systems, including those in England and Wales. The scenarios for assessment are seen as relating to curriculum goals addressed by a pupil (general or specific or both) and various assessment scenarios. Where the pupil follows general educational goals, assessment may consist of participation in all parts of general educational assessment with either: no accommodation, accommodation in some parts or accommodation in all parts.

Where the pupil addresses both general and pupil-specific goals, assessment may comprise participation in some parts of general education assessment either with or without accommodations and alternative assessment for pupil-specific goals. Finally, where the curriculum goals are pupil specific (e.g. to do with independent functioning), the assessment would involve alternative assessment for these goals. These might include portfolio assessment as a way of gathering information on achievement (Ysseldyke *et al.*, 1997). This has some similarities with an approach in England and Wales to the use of Records of Achievement (RoA).

Examples of accommodations for assessment may be summarized in relation to time, setting, presentation and response. Flexible time may include extended time, alternating the lengths of test sessions (e.g. long/ short), more frequent breaks and multiple sessions over several days. Flexible settings may involve testing alone, in small groups, at home with a monitor, in a special educational classroom or in a room with special lighting. Alternative presentation formats could embrace Braille or large print, the signing of directions, paraphrasing, audio- or video-taped directions or highlighted key words. Alternative response formats include pointing to the response, using a template, responding in sign language, using a computer and allowing answers to be made in a test book (Rouse *et al.*, 2000).

Performance-based assessments are increasingly used in the USA, allowing the pupil to show knowledge in a natural context. They may comprise performing a task or preparing a portfolio or an exhibition. Kentucky offer an alternative portfolio for students not working towards the usual diploma. It includes entries showing the student's work in several 'life domains' and a summary of the students job activities and experiences (Kentucky Department of Education, 1996).

Importantly, accommodations for testing should mirror those for teaching and accommodations for a particular pupil should be related to her *particular* educational needs. It should also be recognized that a pupil might require accommodations for some parts of a general educational assessment but not need the same accommodation for other parts (or may need different accommodations). Accommodations are intended to level the playing field for pupils with SEN, not to provide them with preferential treatment (Rouse *et al.*, 2000).

Target-setting

The American essayist Ralph Waldo Emerson believed that nothing great was ever achieved without enthusiasm. In the present day anyone could be forgiven for thinking that society has come to the conclusion that nothing great can be achieved without targets, so great is the plethora of them, from reducing hospital waiting lists to cutting down the cost of photocopying.

Target-setting, benchmarking and value added measures have been long used in industry and commerce, but only more recently have attempts been made to apply some aspects of these approaches to public sector services, including education. The point of setting targets in education and the related issues of benchmarking and value added measures are clearly and explicitly to raise standards.

In England and Wales, strategies for target-setting were developed under the Conservative government and the subsequent Labour government (see OFSTED, 1996; Barber, 1997; Schools Curriculum and Assessment Authority, 1997a,b; DfEE, 1998). Schools are statutorily required to set targets in relation to age and expected level of achievement. This includes the expectation that a pupil at the end of Key Stage 2 of schooling (that is, at 11 years old) would be expected to achieve a specified level (level 4). Students in the final year of secondary schooling (16-year-olds) are expected to achieve certain grades in GCSE examinations or their equivalent. Schools are statutorily required to set targets for the following:

- the percentage of 11-year-old pupils achieving level 4 of the National Curriculum or better in English and mathematics at the end of Key Stage 2;
- the percentage of 16-year-old pupils gaining five or more A* to C grades at GCSE examinations or their equivalent;
- the percentage of 16-year-old pupils gaining one or more A* to G grades at GCSE examinations or their equivalent;
- the average GCSE/GNVQ score per pupil calculated by assigning each grade a number on an ascending numerical scale according to the higher level of the grade.

National targets are set in terms of these levels. It will be seen that these targets are expressed in terms of the achievement of pupils. To support and encourage the setting of school targets, the government has set national targets for the percentage of pupils nationally to reach the various levels listed above. In their turn LEAs set targets for which they are held to account by the government for schools in their areas. Schools themselves agree targets with the LEA. The whole structure is intended to raise standards by challenging LEAs and schools to improve.

Potentially negative effects of target-setting on schools working with pupils with SEN

Colin MacInnes, the novelist, said that England is a country infested with people who love to tell us what to do, but who very rarely seem to know what is going on. Whether this is an unfair way in which to view the present obsession with targets time will tell. But the effect of target-setting is rarely uniformly positive.

There has been an understandable focus on the statutory targets which are published and which journalists and many parents like to see expressed as league tables that purport to indicate the success of the various schools. It has been pointed out that a school performing below national expectations may be doing well with its intake of pupils starting from a lower starting point than other schools. This is of course the 'value added' argument. However, parents looking for the best school for their children may be unimpressed by schools doing comparatively well from a lower starting point. Aspiring parents understandably may be more interested in the schools offering higher standards in more 'absolute' terms.

Consequently, the pressure on schools to raise standards is keenly felt. This has led some schools to focus their attentions particularly on pupils who are at the cusp of the threshold which will show up in the published tables. Primary schools are eager to ensure that the pupils approaching the end of Key Stage 2 (age 11) who are nearing level 4 of the National Curriculum in English and mathematics make it past this winning post. Secondary schools are equally concerned that their pupils at 16 years old who are close to getting five A* to C grade GCSEs (the favoured measure of success) do so.

A point to remember is that whenever targets are set there is a cost, as resources tend to be drawn from other potential areas so that targets may be reached. This is why in industry managers are careful not to set too many targets and use target setting very much as a way of underlining priorities. Targets should be rifle bullets, not spread shot.

The concern is that in education, in seeking to reach statutory targets, schools concentrate time and learning resources on the pupils in the middle band of attainment. This can, if the school is not very careful, lead to resources being drawn away from pupils who have SEN and who would not be expected to reach the expected threshold. This applies less to pupils with more severe SEN, who in England and Wales have statements of special education needs, which attracts considerable funding and more to the pupils whose SEN are less severe but still significant.

Statutory targets as a possible inhibitor of mainstream inclusion

Another effect of the pressures that arise from statutory target setting is that it may make schools reluctant to accept increasing numbers of pupils with SEN. This effect could be encouraged at the very time that the government in the United Kingdom is seeking to increase the inclusion of pupils with SEN into mainstream schools. For example consider a mainstream school taking on to its roll pupils with moderate learning difficulties. These pupils are by definition so far behind others in their standards and progress that they are most unlikely to approach the statutory target threshold and will affect the school's results in the league tables. While the pupils with moderate learning difficulties may make reasonable progress, it would be unlikely to be sufficient to show up in the league tables.

Schools recognize the need to set targets on an assumption that parameters do not change once the targets have been set. If inclusion increases the number of children with SEN in ordinary schools this is likely to have implications for the targets set by the school. Yet there appears to be no machinery for adjusting achievement targets to reflect the inclusion of pupils with SEN.

Target-setting for pupils with SEN

Just as it is important to set targets for the whole school, so it is beneficial to use target-setting for pupils with SEN. If the standards of pupils on the register of SEN (a document listing the names of children in a school identified as having SEN, along with basic information about them) are known, then targets can be set to raise their levels of attainment. For many pupils with literacy difficulties, such targets could be set in terms of levels of literacy. Targets may also be set in terms of other areas of cognitive development and in terms of behaviour and of emotional and social development. For pupils with a disability the target would also be set in terms of achievement, to help to ensure that the arrangements made to give that pupil access to learning and the curriculum were effective.

As with target-setting for all pupils, that for pupils with SEN involves establishing where pupils are at present (Qualifications and Curriculum Authority, 1998). The next step is to establish how the cohort concerned compares with apparently similar cohorts in other schools.

For some pupils with SEN (for example, pupils with behavioural, emotional and social difficulties) the National Curriculum benchmarking data that apply to all pupils may be useful. Making comparisons would involve establishing the attainment levels for the cohort of pupils with such difficulties within the school and comparing these with the levels achieved by similar pupils in other apparently similar schools. For other pupils, for whom National Curriculum levels are not a sufficiently sensitive measure, other scales of attainment may be helpful. One such scale (mentioned above) has been developed by the National Foundation of Educational Research (NFER). This 'p' scale seeks to enable small steps of attainment that are below level 1 of the National Curriculum to be recognized and recorded.

The third step in target-setting is to determine what more the cohort concerned should achieve in a specified time, perhaps a year. Next the school has to take action to reach the targets. The whole process is sometimes presented as a cycle of target setting followed by an assessment of why targets were or were not reached followed by setting new targets.

An important part of the process, indeed the main part, is the strategy that the school uses to help to ensure that the agreed targets are reached, who is responsible for reaching them, where the time and funds and equipment necessary will come from and so on. When the cycle is under way and certainly when it is completed each time, the school will examine which strategies appear to have contributed to success and which were less useful. Care has to be taken where cohorts are very small that inferences are not made which do not have a reasonably secure foundation.

Benchmarking

Although it has some pitfalls, benchmarking can be a useful tool if used wisely. It is not, of course, an ideal solution to anything. To think it is would be to take the sort of idealistic position that led H. L. Menken to observe, 'An idealist is one who, on noticing that a rose smells better than a cabbage, concludes that it will also make better soup.'

Benchmarking (Schools Curriculum and Assessment Authority, 1997b) raises other challenges. In England and Wales, when schools come to compare themselves with supposedly similar schools, the tables that guide the comparisons take into account prior learning and English as an additional language, but not SEN. If benchmarking does not reflect the relative inclusion by different schools of pupils with SEN, it is hard to see how schools otherwise similar but with different levels of inclusion could be fairly compared.

Benchmarking becomes more realistic when schools compare themselves with other schools having similar percentages of pupils on the register of SEN, with comparable levels of learning difficulty and disability. The progress of pupils in such situations may be compared over a specified period of perhaps a year. If one school makes better progress than another which is comparable in terms of initial standards of attainment of pupils on the register of SEN, then the more successful and the less successful schools can be compared to seek to determine the reasons for success.

For example, a small number of broadly similar schools may decide to compare the reading comprehension levels of pupils on their SEN register at an agreed point in time and perhaps six months later. The comparative results should give rise to a productive professional discussion about which factors may be contributing to relative success and which features may be constraining pupil progress.

Value added measures: baseline assessment as an indicator of value added

From a specified starting point, progress can be estimated. Dickens's Little Dorritt was born in the Marshalsea prison as flies swarmed around her mother in the stifling heat, so that the child's life appeared 'among the multitude of lesser deaths'. From this unenviable entry into the world, Little Dorritt was to develop into the young woman who married Arthur Clenham and walked down the steps of St George's Church 'inseparable and blessed'. So the progress of a life can be estimated according to its starting point.

In education, baseline assessment is being developed to extend to pupils who may have SEN. Its use as a value added measure is also being developed (Schools Curriculum and Assessment Authority, 1997c). There was a trailing version of baseline assessment scales for children with special educational needs (Qualifications and Curriculum Authority, 1997). This has very much been overtaken by the development of such assessments as the p scales.

Some schools are concerned that the inclusion of pupils with SEN might adversely affect their overall achievement results. In such instances, baseline assessment may be used as a value added tool and other value added measures may be used to try to address the concern. But it remains to be seen whether these hold as much credibility for parents and others as more 'absolute' measures of achievement.

As pointed out above, some parents select a school not according to value added but on the absolute results achieved, as an indication of the level at which the school is working. Some sections of the media view absolute measures as more newsworthy than value added, which is an altogether more suspect concept to them. With this perspective parents faced with choosing a school for their child would pick a school where children achieved well rather than one in which they had progressed well from a lower starting point.

SUMMARY

Curriculum and assessment can help in the education of pupils with SEN by providing a common framework and a common language in which provision and assessment can be made. Where pupils with SEN do not benefit from the general curriculum and assessments provided for all pupils, efforts are being made to extend the lower levels of the curriculum and to provide smaller steps to learning, so that progress can take place. In assessment, accommodations are made to the general curriculum to try to provide opportunities for pupils with SEN to demonstrate what they have achieved. Where different curricula and different assessments are necessary, it will be important to develop these to provide consistency of approach so that comparisons can be made of pupil standards and progress.

Target-setting and the related issues of benchmarking and value added measures are becoming increasingly accepted in relation to the large cohorts of pupils in schools. These large cohorts are compared with both the national school population and, more helpfully, schools estimated to be similar on such measures as social deprivation indicators.

There are potentially negative effects of target-setting according to national expectations. To reach such targets, schools may feel under pressure to divert resources from pupils with SEN (and from very able pupils) to the middle achieving pupils most likely to reach the thresholds of the targets concerned. Target-setting for all pupils may inhibit the mainstream inclusion of pupils with SEN where the standards of attainment of such pupils are lower than the national expectations (e.g. pupils with moderate learning difficulties).

Target-setting for pupils with SEN has developed more slowly than that for all pupils. Benchmarking and consequently value added measures for pupils with SEN are being developed so that they are more securely established. Baseline assessment is a helpful tool in contributing to target-setting, benchmarking and value added measures because it allows schools to assess the progress made from a comparable starting point in different schools.

If such starting points in schools can be determined, the schools can be usefully compared according to the degree to which they contribute to pupil progress and consequently to improved standards of pupil achievement. In the case of pupils with SEN the role of standards of achievement is important once again in being the starting point for target-setting and in being central to benchmarking and value added measures. This applies whether the attainment is related to learning difficulties or whether it is a pragmatic indicator of the effectiveness of provision which aims to ensure access to learning and the curriculum for disabled pupils.

References

Barber, M. (1997) 'Target setting and school improvement – the way forward'. Letter to all chief education officers in England, 21 July.

DfEE (1997a) *Excellence in Schools*. London: Department for Education and Employment.

DfEE (1997b) *Excellence for All Children: Meeting Special Educational Needs*. London: Department for Education and Employment.

DfEE (1998) *Supporting the Target Setting Process: Guidance for Effective Target Setting for Pupils with Special Educational Needs.* London: Department for Education and Employment.

DfEE (1999a) *The National Curriculum Handbook for Primary Teachers in England.* London: Department of Education and Employment/Qualifications and Curriculum Authority.

DfEE (1999b) *The National Curriculum Handbook for Secondary Teachers in England.* London: Department for Education and Employment/Qualifications and Curriculum Authority.

Goertz, M. E. and Friedman, D. H. (1996) 'State education reform and students with disabilities: a preliminary analysis'. In *Year 1 Technical Report, Centre for Policy Research on the Impact of General and Special Education Reform.* Alexandria, VA: National Association of State Boards of Education.

Kentucky Department of Education (1996) *KRISS: Kentucky Alternative Portfolio Project Teachers' Guide.* Lexington: Kentucky Systems Change Project for Students with Severe Disabilities.

McLaughlin, M. J. and Tilstone, C. (2000) 'Standards and the curriculum', in M. J. McLaughlin and M. Rouse (eds) *Special Education and School Reform in the United States and Britain.* London: Routledge.

OFSTED (1996) *Setting Targets to Raise Standards: A Survey of Good Practice.* London: Office for Standards in Education/Department for Education and Employment.

Qualifications and Curriculum Authority (1997) *Baseline Assessment Scales for Children with Special Educational Needs: Teachers' Guide.* London: QCA.

Qualifications and Curriculum Authority (1998) *Supporting the Target Setting Process: Guidance for Effective Target Setting for Pupils with Special Educational Needs.* London: QCA, Standards and Effectiveness Unit and Department of Education and Employment.

Rouse, M. and Agbenu, R. (1998) 'Assessment and special educational needs: teachers' dilemmas'. *British Journal of Special Education,* **25**(2), 81–7.

Rouse, M., Shiner, J. G. and Danielson, L. (2000) 'National assessment and special education in the United States and England and Wales', in M. J. McLaughlin and M. Rouse (eds) *Special Education and School Reform in the United States and Great Britain.* London: Routledge.

Schools Curriculum and Assessment Authority (1997a) *Value Added Indicators for Schools.* London: SCAA.

Schools Curriculum and Assessment Authority (1997b) *Target Setting and Benchmarking for Schools: Consultation Paper.* London: SCAA.

Schools Curriculum and Assessment Authority (1997c) *Baseline Assessment Scales.* London: SCAA.

Teacher Training Agency (1997) *Consultation Paper on National Standards for Special Educational Needs Co-ordinators.* London: TTA.

Ysseldyke, J. E., Olsen, K. and Thurslow, M. L. (1997) *Issues and Considerations in Alternative Assessments.* Minneapolis: National Centre on Educational Research, University of Minnesota.

CHAPTER 4

Inclusion

Introduction

Oscar Wilde said, 'Education is an admirable thing, but it is well to remember from time to time that nothing that is worth knowing can be taught.' Less caustically, the American financier E. A. Filene said, 'When a man's education is finished, he is finished.' This last sentiment is why it is so important that as many as possible are included in the remit of education. The difficulty arises when there are different views of what it means to be included.

This chapter considers various definitions of inclusion. It argues for an approach to inclusion that takes into account the standards of pupil achievement demonstrated by the venue where the education is to take place. This approach is called 'educational inclusion' (Farrell, 2000b).

Defining inclusion

The term inclusion has come to mean different things in different contexts, so it is worth trying to establish a definition. One starting point is to distinguish 'inclusion' from 'integration'. Both terms are to do with the provision for pupils with SEN in mainstream schools. Integration assumes that the mainstream school system remains the same but that extra arrangements are made to provide for pupils with SEN.

Inclusion aims to encourage schools to reconsider their structure, teaching approaches, pupil grouping and use of support so that the school responds to the needs of all pupils. Teachers seek to develop opportunities to look at new ways of involving all pupils and to draw on experimentation and reflection. Collaboration is important. There should be planned access to a broad and balanced curriculum developed from its foundations as a curriculum for all pupils. Inclusive education is pertinent for all schools, including special schools (Farrell, 2000a).

In England and Wales, a rather restricted view of inclusion was taken by the Green Paper *Excellence for All Children: Meeting Special Educational Needs* published in October 1997 (DfEE, 1997b). It concerns raising standards, shifting resources to practical support and increasing inclusion. Building on views expressed in an earlier consultation paper (Kilfoyle, 1997) and signalled by the White Paper *Excellence in Schools* (DfEE, 1997a), the Green Paper seeks to set the future direction of special education.

Yet the document gives no explicit and coherent definition of inclusion such as those found elsewhere (e.g. Clarke, C. *et al.*, 1995). Further confusion is evident, as the earlier consultation paper (Kilfoyle, 1997) uses the terms 'inclusion' and 'integration' interchangeably. The Green Paper view appears to be that inclusion applies only to children being included in an ordinary school rather than a special school. This suggests that to place a pupil in a special school is to exclude, and there is an interesting parallel here with the debate about whether the special school offers a 'least restrictive environment' for certain pupils. This concept has long been used in the USA, where the appropriate education required by federal law has to be put together for individual pupils to meet the particular needs of the child and be provided in the least restrictive environment.

The Qualifications and Curriculum Authority (Wade, 1999) takes the view that inclusion means 'securing appropriate opportunities for learning, assessment and qualifications to enable the full and effective participation of all pupils in the process of learning'.

Social inclusion

The UK government's approach to social inclusion is reflected in Circulars 10/99 (DfEE, 1999a) and 11/99 (DfEE, 1999b).

Circular 10/99 highlights the need to provide for pupils in school rather than by excluding them. Among ways of cutting down exclusions from school are seeking to reduce disaffection in particular among pupils in known high-risk categories, such as those with SEN who may develop challenging behaviour. Another at-risk group is pupils whose attainments tend to be very low. Approaches to such pupils include early intervention, careful planning and whole-school approaches. School-based pastoral support programmes (PSP) are developed with the help of external services for pupils who are at serious risk of permanent exclusion or of being drawn into criminal behaviour. For pupils who already have Individual Education Plans, these IEPs should be made to encompass the features of a PSP. Normally a PSP will be put in operation and will have failed before the school resorts to exclusion. Once a pupil is excluded, the headteacher and the LEA should plan for his or her reintegration into school based education.

Circular 11/99 concerns the LEA's role in supporting pupils. It emphasizes that pupils excluded for more than three weeks should get a fulltime suitable alternative education. LEAs and other agencies should work to reduce exclusions in line with a national target. The LEA must consider compelling attendance through legal remedies and should support schools that have pupils with PSPs.

Of particular relevance to social exclusion and pupils with SEN is that pupils with statements of SEN appear to be seven times more likely to be excluded than pupils without statements, the figures being respectively 0.98 and 0.14 per cent (Donovan, 1998). While this is of concern, a contribution to the increased rate is pupils with statements relating to behavioural, emotional and social difficulties, which may be associated with their conduct being detrimental to the education of others, consequently leading to their exclusion.

Inclusion in the USA

In the 1960s and the 1970s, civil rights proponents worked to lay down the principle that a child with a disability should be seen as having the same right to access to education as a non-disabled child. State and local authorities, in order to receive federal funds for special education, must provide all children with disabilities with a free appropriate education in the least restrictive environment. Each child is given protection through procedural due process to help to ensure that the goals of the Individuals with Disabilities Education Act (IDEA) are met.

Full inclusion

The expression 'full inclusion' indicates that all pupils with SEN should be educated in mainstream schools. A range of provision in which SEN could be met (such as mainstream school, special school and home teaching) would not be acceptable. It would be better to have increased support and resources in mainstream schools in proportion to the severity and complexity of the SEN (Gartner and Lipsky, 1989).

The Green Paper does not support full inclusion but still speaks of 'strong educational as well as social and moral grounds for educating children with SEN with their peers' (p. 43). More realistically, the Green Paper states that 'parents will continue to have a right to express a preference for a special school' (Chapter 4, para. 4). The government document *Meeting Special Educational Needs: a Programme of Action* (DfEE, 1998) continues this theme. An important point is that where possible even if pupils are not placed in mainstream schools they should spend as much time as possible in mainstream settings (DfEE, 1998, Chapter 3, para. 5).

Some reservations about unqualified inclusion

The American politician Warren Austin perhaps took matters too far when he suggested that 'The Jews and the Arabs should sit down and settle their differences like good Christians', but differences can be fruitful starting points for seeking a clearer view of a subject. It is not difficult to differ with the government's view of education because it is so confused. It is as if government wants the idealism of full inclusion and at the same time the pragmatism of constrained inclusion.

The exemplars of good practice given in the Green Paper in the chapter on inclusion are superficial and say nothing about how inclusion has raised the standards of the pupils concerned. If the aim of the Green Paper is to raise standards, then surely a key part of any decision to include a pupil in an ordinary school would involve demonstrating that standards would be raised to greater degree than if the pupil were placed in a special school.

There is no indication of what is meant by the government wanting 'more children' with SEN included in ordinary schools. It is quite proper that this is left to interpretation so that local circumstances can inform judgements about inclusion. It would surely be a retrograde step if later the government attempted to use benchmarking to produce tables of the most inclusive local education authorities and encourage those who were less inclusive to emulate the others. This would ignore whether local special schools were excellent or poor and would not take account of the standards achieved by schools in inclusive authorities.

Nowhere in the Green Paper does it say that children presently in special schools should be in ordinary schools. Is the intention that in the future, when a child's placement is considered, more credence should be given to a placement in an ordinary school? This seems to imply that present judgements have insufficiently considered the needs of the child. It is unclear in what different ways the needs of the child should be considered in the future if this is to lead to more placements in ordinary schools.

It is stated that 'The ultimate purpose of special educational needs provision is to enable young people to flourish in adult life. There are therefore strong educational, as well as social and moral grounds for educating children with special educational needs with their peers' (p. 43). This implies that where a special school has been chosen, some moral imperative has been given insufficient credence. Yet the possibility that there might be educational, social and moral grounds for educating children with SEN in a special school is not considered.

In the particular case of including pupils with emotional and behavioural difficulties (Chapter 8) in an ordinary school, an issue arises if a teacher has particular difficulty coping. Given such a situation the grounds for competency procedures against the teacher become complicated. The approach of school inspectors to such a situation could presumably not take too much account of the pupil's disturbance.

The Green Paper says that parental choice will include maintaining parents' present right to express a preference for a special school place for their child where they believe it necessary (Chapter 2: Working with parents). But it is not clear what this means. There may be a distinction between a parent expressing a choice and that choice being granted or recognized. If parental choice is not accepted, there will have to be criteria for acceptance or rejection.

Parents will have a right to express a preference for a special school 'where they consider it appropriate to their child's needs'. But all those involved will need to be careful to avoid a bias towards the more articulate parents, perhaps from a more privileged background, being able to express their preference more effectively than other parents. There could be a role here for parent support groups to help to ensure equity. There is an important role here for independent parent supporters and parent partnership officers of the LEA.

It is said that children should be enrolled in ordinary schools unless there are 'compelling reasons' for doing otherwise. It is not yet apparent how this relates to parental preference for a special school. Whether the expression of a parental preference constitutes a 'compelling reason' remains to be seen.

'Facts are like ventriloquists' dummies,' said Aldous Huxley. 'Sitting on a wise man's knee they may be made to utter words of wisdom: elsewhere they say nothing or talk nonsense.' In a similar way, the constituent parts of a school are sometimes like these facts which have been made to speak coherently in one setting but cannot necessarily be forced to make sense in another. The provision of a special school seems to be understood as comprising the skills of staff (Chapter 6), which can be exercised in other settings or which can be conveyed to teachers in ordinary schools.

This 'skills and competencies' approach is reflected in Teacher Training Agency documents, including those relating to special educational needs. The document relating to special educational needs coordinators, for example, sets out in a systematic but potentially mechanistic way the key outcomes of SEN coordination, professional knowledge and understanding, skills and attributes and key areas of SEN coordination (Teacher Training Agency, 1998).

But there are aspects of special schools integral to the whole school. Examples of these are the boundaries, both physical and psychological, of a good special school (especially for children with behavioural, emotional and social difficulties) and the concentration of staff expertise built upon by regular contact with other highly skilled colleagues. Other examples are the close monitoring of pupils made possible by the small class sizes in special schools and the location of specialist staff among a group of children who need their services. There is surely also a meaningful sense in which one can talk about inclusion in a special school. Inclusion in a special school where a child's needs are met can lead to greater inclusion in society in later life for the young person. Being in a mainstream school where needs are not being met is inclusion in only a cosmetic sense.

Related to the notion of teacher skills, much care needs to be taken over the type and extent of training to help to enskill a teacher in an ordinary school to teach pupils with perhaps different and more complex special educational needs than previously. A reductionist model of skills, knowledge and experience does not seem suitable for such a situation, but some kind of structure is necessary for training.

One approach would be to develop placements in special schools for teachers in ordinary schools so that they can develop practice with a mentor and the whole-school support framework of a good special school. Different stages of teacher training and education might introduce involvement with good special schools on a continuum. These might begin with visits and team teaching in special schools in early initial teacher training. They could develop into teaching in a special school as part of the professional development of a well established ordinary school teacher.

Meeting Special Educational Needs: a Programme of Action (DfEE, 1998) includes a timetable summarizing action over the three years following its publication. The *Programme* builds on the Green Paper *Excellence for All Children*.

Government intended to promote further inclusion and develop the role of special schools. From 1999, LEAs would publish information about their policy on inclusion in their Education Development Plans. The statutory framework for inclusion (section 316 of the Education Act 1996) would be reviewed. Government would identify and disseminate good practice by special schools in developing practical links with mainstream schools. The contribution of special schools to an increasingly inclusive education system would be promoted. Steps would be taken to ensure that children with SEN are treated fairly in schools' admissions procedures. Financial support would be provided for projects aiming to improve provision and raise achievements for children with emotional and behavioural difficulties.

'Educational inclusion' and standards

An important aim of the Green Paper is to raise standards. Consequently, a key part of any consideration to include a pupil in mainstream school would be an indication that a direct result would be the raising of the pupil's standard of attainment. This level would be equal to or beyond that which would be achieved were the pupil placed in a special school or other setting (Farrell, 1998). Such a judgement would also apply to the proportion of time in which a pupil was educated in a mainstream school and that in which he or she was educated in a special school or elsewhere.

'Educational inclusion' (Farrell, 2000b) seeks to take into account the importance both of inclusion and of raising the standards achieved by pupils with SEN. The concept of mainstream inclusion should be modified to one of 'educational inclusion' in order to avoid the impression that for 'mainstream inclusion' there is an implication that venues other than mainstream schools are inferior. The placement of pupils with SEN could be informed by the effectiveness of the setting in raising the attainment of pupils in terms of educational, personal and social attainment.

Placement in a mainstream school, special school, education at home or elsewhere could be informed by evidence (possibly ongoing) that the placement raised a pupil's standards of attainment. If it did not, an alternative venue could be considered. One approach to encouraging this could be through parents being informed of the standards achieved by particular venues. Of course, this does not preclude improving the standards in the particular mainstream school until the standards exceed those of, say, a special school and then increasing inclusion in the mainstream school. There is some evidence (from performance tables in 1997) that schools developing greater inclusion can at the same time raise examination results. If this does occur it may involve teachers learning to teach all pupils more effectively as they hone their skills to meet the greater diversity of the school population (Sebba and Ainscow, 1996).

Raising standards (rather than the in-built assumption that mainstream school is the preferred venue on human rights grounds) would inform placements. Such an approach is called 'educational inclusion' to distinguish it from 'mainstream' inclusion, which assumes the superiority of mainstream schooling. The judgement of the appropriateness of a venue for teaching pupils with learning difficulty would be informed by the following.

1. The quality of teaching in the setting concerned (for example, mainstream school, special school, home education). Care would be necessary in judging this. For example, if teaching is satisfactory or better, then low standards of pupil achievement and slow progress may relate to factors other than school ones. These might include deprived family circumstances that have led to low standards of attainment of pupils starting at school. Such family circumstances may contribute to a pupil making slow progress despite satisfactory or better teaching because negative approaches and attitudes to

learning may be ingrained. Where standards of pupil attainment are low and progress is slow while teaching is satisfactory or better, this is an indication that the pupil concerned has learning difficulties. Where standards of pupil attainment are low and progress is slow, while teaching is unsatisfactory or worse, this is an indication of a poor school. This does not necessarily indicate that some pupils may not also have learning difficulties. Further, the quality of teaching which may have contributed to low standards and slow progress of pupils may not be that which the pupils are experiencing currently, but may be the result of poor teaching at an earlier time.

2. The progress made by pupils in academic performance and in personal and social development, judged by assessing initial and subsequent attainment; for example, using the p scales and National Curriculum level descriptions for personal, social and health education.

3. The standards of academic, social and personal attainment reached by pupils with broadly similar levels of initial attainment in different local venues.

Such criteria would help to determine the child's placement and justify its continuation as appropriate. The evidence for these standards would be indicated, for example, by: school inspectors' reports on mainstream schools and special schools; the self-monitoring of a school; or the judgement of an impartial adviser regarding home teaching.

As the law presently stands, however, a parent may be made aware, say by an LEA, of the respective standards achieved by a mainstream school and a special school. The evidence may indicate that the standards are lower at the present time in the mainstream school and that the child is likely to make slower progress academically, socially and personally in the mainstream school. Given all this, the parent still has the right to express a preference for the mainstream school. The reverse is also the case if standards are lower in a special school than in a mainstream school.

SUMMARY

Inclusion was defined and distinguished from 'integration'. Integration assumes that the mainstream school system is unchanged, while arrangements are made to provide for pupils with SEN. Inclusion implies more fundamental changes and schools are encouraged to examine their structure, teaching approaches and other matters to help to ensure that they are responsive to the needs of all pupils.

Social inclusion involves among other things seeking ways to reduce pupil exclusions from schools by providing support, particularly for at-risk pupils.

In England and Wales, the government view, as indicated in the Green Paper (DfEE, 1997b), appears to be that inclusion applies only to children being included in mainstream school. The Green Paper does not support 'full inclusion' but still considers that there are strong educational, social and moral grounds 'for educating children with SEN with their peers'. Some weaknesses in this position were discussed.

'Educational inclusion' is an approach which takes into account the standards of pupil achievement reached in different venues when considering the appropriate place for a child to be educated. The venues include mainstream school, special school, pupil referral units and home education.

Putting standards of achievement centre stage is likely to reduce the squabbling from the wings of those who are pro- or anti-inclusion by introducing onto the scene something other than strong conviction.

References

Barber, M. (1997) 'Target setting and school improvement – the way forward. Letter to all chief education officers in England, 21 July.

Clarke, C., Dawson, A. and Millward, A. (eds) (1995) *Towards Inclusive Schooling*. London: David Fulton.

DfEE (1997a) *Excellence in Schools*. London: Department for Education and Employment.

DfEE (1997b) *Excellence for All Children: Meeting Special Educational Needs*. London: Department for Education and Employment.

DfEE (1998) *Meeting Special Educational Needs: a Programme of Action*. London: Department of Education and Employment.

DfEE (1999a) *Circular 10/99. Social Inclusion – Pupil Support*. London: Department for Education and Employment.

DfEE (1999a) *Circular 11/99. Social Inclusion – the LEA Role in Pupil Support*. London: Department for Education and Employment.

Donovan, N. (ed.) (1998) *Second Chances: Exclusion from School and Equality of Opportunities*. London: New Policy Institute.

Farrell, M. (1998) 'Notes on the Green Paper: an initial response'. *British Journal of Special Education*, **25**(1), March.

Farrell, M. (2000a) *Special Education Handbook*, 2nd edn. London: David Fulton.

Farrell, M. (2000b) 'Educational inclusion and raising standards'. *British Journal of Special Education*, **27**(1), 35–8.

Gartner, A. and Lipsky, D. K. (1989) 'New conceptualisations for special education'. *European Journal of Special Needs Education*, 4(1), 16–21.

Kilfoyle, P. (1997) *Every Child is Special: Proposals to Improve Special Needs Education*. London: Labour Party.

OFSTED (1996) *Setting Targets to Raise Standards: a Survey of Good Practice*.

London: Office for Standards in Education/Department for Education and Employment.

Qualifications and Curriculum Authority (1997) *Baseline Assessment Scales for Children with Special Educational Needs: Teachers' Guide*. London: QCA.

Schools Curriculum and Assessment Authority (1997a) *Value Added Indicators for Schools*. London: SCAA.

Schools Curriculum and Assessment Authority (1997b) *Target Setting and Benchmarking for Schools: Consultation Paper*. London: SCAA.

Schools Curriculum and Assessment Authority (1997c) *Baseline Assessment Scales*. London: SCAA.

Sebba, J. and Ainscow, M. (1996) 'International developments in inclusive schooling: mapping the issues'. *Cambridge Journal of Education*, **26**, 5–18.

Teach Training Agency (1997) *Consultation Paper on National Standards for Special Educational Needs Co-ordinators*. London: TTA.

Wade, J. (1999) 'Including all learners: QCA's approach. *British Journal of Special Education*, **26**(2), 80–2.

CHAPTER 5

Special education funding according to levels of achievement

Introduction

People's affection for money is widely recognized. Dr Samuel Johnson said to William Strachan that 'There are few ways in which a man can be more innocently employed than in getting money.' Much more recently a generous attitude to wealth is suggested in the comedian Spike Milligan's remark, 'Money can't buy you friends, but you can get a better class of enemy.'

This chapter is about money. It explains the national and local arrangements for targeting resources for SEN in England and Wales. If pupils with SEN are to be provided for appropriately, it is important that resources are commensurately increased for those with the more severe SEN. One element in determining this is by reference to the standards of achievement reached by pupils. A mechanism using common achievement data is therefore useful to produce greater equity and better targeting of at least some element of resources.

The rise and rise of special education funding

In both the USA and England and Wales, concern has been expressed about the rising costs of SEN. In the USA, Parrish (1997) has intimated that the increase in funding for SEN is encroaching on the overall funding available for public sector education. Researchers at the National Foundation for Educational Research in England have drawn attention to increasing special education budgets, which in some LEAs have contributed to overspending (Fletcher-Campbell, 1996).

Among ways of controlling expenditure on SEN is that indicated in a report by a firm of accountants who conducted research for a group of LEAs in England and Wales (Coopers and Lybrand, 1996). If expenditure is to be kept constant by LEAs, either the 'unit value' of the component of funding relating to pupils with SEN has to be reduced or the unit value of the component for pupils without SEN must be reduced. In other words, if the number of pupils with SEN increases, either each gets proportionately less funding or pupils who do not have SEN get proportionately less.

While this would help to keep expenditure under control and predictable, such an approach does not assure the fair distribution of resources. For example, particular schools may seek to identify greater and greater numbers of pupils with SEN, perhaps with the support of parents, representatives of voluntary bodies and others without any serious long-term reflection on the consequences for other schools and children.

National allocation of funds in England and Wales

Formulae are not invariably helpful. Aldous Huxley pointed out that you learn to love by loving and 'there isn't any formula or method.' While we may get away with this in matters like love, with something as important as money in education formulae for allocating funds are taken seriously.

In England and Wales, the Department for Education and Employment indicates what it expects individual LEAs to spend based on a national formula called the Standard Spending Assessment. This notionally distributes the available funding to all LEAs. In practice, each local authority spends at a level determined by its councillors (locally elected politicians). This is broadly funded from the council tax, national non-domestic rates and the revenue support grant. The council tax is a local tax for services. National non-domestic rates are a pooled national business rate where local authorities are entitled to an amount per head of population, rather than a share of what they have actually collected. The revenue support grant is directed funding for local authorities from central government.

Principally, the funding is distributed on the basis of pupil numbers, but there are other factors relating to different costs of living in different regions, population sparsity and additional educational needs (AEN). The AEN element is predominantly based on indices of social deprivation: the number of lone parent families, proportions of the community from ethnic minority backgrounds and of pupils eligible for free school meals.

With reference to the indicator of free school meals, the families of children who are eligible to have free school meals are in the lowest income brackets, and this is taken to be associated with deprivation and lower educational achievement. Some families who are eligible for free school meals may be reticent to let this be known because they fear social stigma, so eligibility estimates may be inaccurate.

This approach to the distribution of funds could be viewed as indicating that the DfEE is drawing strong parallels between social deprivation and SEN. However, across LEAs there may be no reason to adjust for SEN because the most likely situation is that pupils with the most severe SEN are evenly distributed across England and Wales. (These are the roughly 3 per cent that have a legal document of entitlement called a Statement of SEN.) However, this macro view does not imply that schools will have a uniform distribution of such pupils.

The fact that different LEAs have substantially different proportions of pupils with Statements of SEN does not disprove this theory. Instead, it may highlight the different local practices, most importantly the point at which an individual pupil's SEN trigger the assessment process that may lead to a Statement of SEN. The DfEE has avoided the use of subjective data in the Standard Spending Assessment because it recognizes that they can produce perverse incentives.

Local allocation of funds in England and Wales

'Money is like a sixth sense,' said the novelist and short story writer W. Somerset Maugham, 'without which you cannot make complete use of the other five.' In a similar vein, Horace advised, 'by right means if you can, but by any means make money.' Money is as important to local authorities as to any other organization.

In England and Wales, LEA expenditure on SEN covers a range of factors. Costs *not* delegated to mainstream schools may include:

- educational psychologists;
- special support services who work with pupils at the 'action plus' aspect of the *Code of Practice* (pupils who require extra support from outside the school but not a Statement of SEN);
- educational welfare officers (although their work covers other pupils who do not have SEN);
- 'out borough' pupils, i.e. pupils who attend schools outside the funding LEA, such as day or residential special schools;
- pupils who attend the LEA's own special schools;
- cost of Statements for pupils in mainstream schools;
- special resourced units in mainstream schools for particular areas of SEN, such as hearing impairment;
- units and support for pupils excluded from schools (although not all these pupils may have SEN);
- administration costs such as that for the writing and maintaining of Statements of SEN;
- transport for pupils with SEN.

Funds are also delegated to schools and may comprise:

- Non-specific funds for SEN allocated according to a formula based on the number of pupils and their age. Accountants Coopers and Lybrand (1996) estimated this to represent between 5.3 and 16.6 per cent of the overall unit of funding.

- Funds allocated through a proxy indicator, such as pupil eligibility for free school meals.
- Funds allocated according to an audit of SEN or by some other means.

Presently, as the local intermediary, the LEA allocates funds to schools for pupils with SEN. This may be done in several ways.

1. Some funds may be directed to SEN support services that seek to give support according to levels of 'need' across local schools. These centrally funded services are accessed in different degrees by different schools.
2. Funds for pupils with statements of SENs are directed to the school.
3. Some funds are allocated according to a formula based on the number of pupils and their age (this is sometimes called the age-weighted pupil unit, or AWPU). This element of formula funding is 'opaque' and it is not possible to point to the particular component of the AWPU and demonstrate that it is the element for SEN. The AWPU argument is based on the principle that the basic level of funding received by schools ought to be sufficient to meet the needs of pupils within a reasonable range. It assumes that this can be done without the school needing to receive additional support (whether for pupils with Statements of SEN or for those with SEN but without Statements).
4. Some funds may be distributed by the LEA to local schools via a formula that depends on the 'levels' of SEN in each school (related to the *SEN Code of Practice*).

In short, the approach recognizes a continuum of SEN matched by a continuum of support and funding. This assumes, however, that the different 'levels' of SEN are meaningful and comparable.

Statements of SEN

Guarantees of anything have to be examined very carefully. In his charming play *Blythe Spirit*, Noel Coward has a character say, 'We have no reliable guarantee that the after life will be any less exasperating than this one.' Despite reservations about reassurances in general, it has become widely accepted that in England and Wales the closest one can get to a guarantee of suitable provision for SEN is a Statement of SEN.

In England and Wales just under 3 per cent of pupils have Statements of SEN (DfEE, 1997b). The LEA is responsible for identifying the needs of pupils with SEN who require a Statement and for providing the additional resources that are required to meet their needs. The Statement provides the legal entitlement for the pupil to receive the provision outlined in the Statement, and the LEA has the legal responsibility to ensure that the provision specified in the Statement is provided. While the funding may be delegated to schools, the LEA still has the legal responsibility to ensure that the provision is received. This may be in the form of extra equipment, additional support, specialist teaching or therapies such as speech and language therapy, where the therapist concerned may be employed not by the LEA but by the local health authority.

Costs to the LEA include that of producing and reviewing the Statement. Potential costs also arise if a parent appeals against decisions of an LEA relating to a Statement's specification of school placement or the provision. A special court, the SEN Tribunal, hears cases and the LEA has to meet costs of preparing the defence, travel for staff, opportunity costs for the use of staff time and the cost of making the arrangements determined by the tribunal.

In England and Wales, where pupils are formally identified as having a significant SEN (by a 'Statement of SEN' attracting extra funding) there is a disincentive for schools and parents to have such funding ended. There may therefore be a discouragement to allowing Statements of SEN to be rescinded. One way of addressing this in the case of learning difficulties, but perhaps less so in the case of disabilities, is to have targets against which a Statement of SENs would be relinquished if the target were reached. These 'exit strategies' would assume that once the pupil had reached a level of achievement which was a little higher than the level which precipitated a Statement being considered in the first place, it would be appropriate to consider rescinding the Statement and reduce the funding to a lower level.

Difficulties with school-based contextual judgements of SEN and the benefits of 'objective' criteria

A Jesuit of my acquaintance pointed out a useful distinction to be made about simplicity. I fear I may have been going on rather about simplifying matters for the sake of clarity when we were discussing some complex issue in the Farm Street headquarters of the Society of Jesus in London. His comment was that 'We should be careful to distinguish between the simplicity of superficiality and the simplicity of depth.'

Simplicity has much to commend it in the distribution of funding, especially with the current concern over transparency in funding. Different LEAs distribute funding for pupils with less severe SEN (that are not associated with Statements) in different ways. One approach is simply to allocate the funds from central government according to the number of pupils eligible for free school meals in each school. Another is to distribute the funding according to the level of SEN that the school itself identifies. This allows the school to determine SEN within the context of its own school, and not according to locally agreed criteria. At the same time, if funds are allocated according to the number of pupils with SEN and the supposed level of significance of the SEN, this system offers a perverse incentive to identify increasing numbers of pupils with SEN and increasing levels of severity in any particular school. It will be remembered that under legislation in England and Wales, SEN is defined in part according to the pupil having a learning difficulty greater than children of the same age.

A difficulty has arisen in recent years in the way in which this definition has been interpreted. SEN may be seen in relation to the context of the child's school. A child may attend a school where pupils attain high standards. Compared with these peers he may have a learning difficulty because his standard of attainment is lower than others' and his progress is slow. A child attending another school where pupil attainment is lower may not be considered to have learning difficulties. Yet the second child may be attaining at a lower level (say in literacy) than the first child and may also be making slow progress. The first, higher attaining, child attracts support and funding and the second child does not. Such anomalies may lead to distribution of funds and support (say by a LEA) which is not commensurate to the level of learning difficulty and the rate of progress made by pupils.

Where schools make contextual judgements about the children with SEN in the school, these relate to the level of skills of the teacher and other school factors as much as the difficulties which the child experiences. This leads to inequities in the number of children who are considered to have SEN in various schools which on the face of it appear quite similar. Where schools are paid more according to the number of children with SEN they have, there is an incentive to identify children and a disincentive to relinquish funds once they are acquired.

Another more justifiable approach is to allocate funds according to some locally agreed definition of SEN involving objective criteria relating to achievement. If standards of educational achievement are used to inform the allocation of resources from LEAs to individual schools, this avoids encouraging schools to identify greater numbers of pupils with SEN. But it is important that this is not seen as simply rewarding schools who have low standards of pupil achievement. Where low standards of pupil achievement relate to the intake of the school, extra funding for SEN can be justified. If, however, the low standards of achievement appear to relate to poor quality of teaching, this needs to be recognized. In such a school the combination of low pupil achievement and poor teaching should pre-cipitate concern about the quality of provision that the school offers.

A continuum of provision for a continuum of need

A matching of action and consequence may be rather roughly indicated in the famous passage from Deuteronomy: 'Eye for eye, tooth for tooth, hand for hand, foot for foot.' More subtly, a general and justifiable principle regarding SEN is to recognize the range of significance and severity of SEN and to seek to match this with a range of resources commensurate with the level of SEN. The assumption is that there is a continuum in mainstream schools, where increasing levels of severity of SEN are met by increasing levels of support.

In England and Wales, the government Green Paper *Excellence for All Children: Meeting Special Educational Needs* (DfEE, 1997b) and the subse-quent document *Meeting Special Educational Needs: a Programme of Action* (DfEE, 1998) both assume a continuum of provision to match a continuum of SEN.

It seems sensible that, in order to raise the standards of achievement of pupils with SEN, one should be clear about what those standards cur-rently are and ensure that they are comparable. The *Programme of Action* points out that 'some studies suggest that we identify significantly more children as having SEN than most other European countries'. It recog-nizes that 'schools and LEAs undoubtedly interpret the term [SEN] in different ways'. It proposes to 'seek to establish a more common under-standing of the provision that is appropriate to meet different levels of SEN' (Chapter 2, para. 3). This approach defines the level of SEN by the level of support 'appropriate' to meet it. It does not explain, however, how the appropriateness of the support is determined. Presumably, it is judged according to the level of SEN, but the determination of this level is not clear. This brings one back to the importance of determining the standards of achievement of pupils with SEN. It is important is this respect that the *SEN Code* (DfEE, 2000a) appends guidance on 'SEN thresholds' (DfEE, 2000b) to aid good practice in decision-making on the identification and provision for pupils with SEN. This includes, for dif-ferent areas of SEN, indications of higher and lower levels of difficulty. For example, in the case of general learning difficulties one indicator for the higher level of difficulty is 'performance within the National Curricu-lum outside the range within which most children are expected to work (i.e. level W at the end of KS1; level 1 at KS2; level 2 at KS3)'.

The *Programme for Action* mentions that the Green Paper (DfEE, 1997b) had invited views on the possibility of 'national criteria for state-ments or for each stage of the *Code of Practice*' (Chapter 2, para. 7). An obstacle to such national criteria, however, is recognized: 'LEAs' discretion over the balance between funding for SEN delegated to schools and that held centrally is an important determinant of the point at which a statement becomes necessary.' This prejudges whether the point at which a statement 'becomes necessary' is consistent across LEAs. The *Programme for Action* (Chapter 2, para. 17) considers that it would not be feasible to set statutory national criteria for statements and chooses instead to publish non-statutory guidance.

In considering improving information about school achievements, the *Programme* points out that LEAs must publish 'core data on the schools in their areas, including the number of pupils with SEN on roll' (Chapter 3, para. 13). Where the judgement about which pupils are on the SEN register lies with the individual school, and given that this judgement can be contextual to the school, it is difficult to see how this information would be useful in initially judging pupil achievement or subsequently assessing progress.

Returning to the issue of a continuum of support, as part of the range of increasing support, there is an implication that there is normally a parallel range of increasing funding. If this funding is to be fairly and equitably distributed, then greater funds should normally be directed towards pupils with greater levels of SEN. For this to be reliable, it is necessary that the national and local distribution of money provides funding matched to the SEN.

Funding for SEN in the USA

In the USA, federal government provides a comparatively small percentage of SEN funding (about 8 per cent in the late 1990s). The remaining funding is borne about equally by the state and the local school districts. The percentage of pupils receiving special education varies considerably from state to state (US Department of Education, 1997). As is the case in England and Wales, it is likely that variations may reflect different practices in identification and provision rather than 'real' differences in the incidence of SEN.

Federal funding relates to the number of children with disabilities in each state who are being provided with special education services, with a 'ceiling' of 12 per cent of the number of school aged children in the state concerned. All states have elements of their funding formulae which allocate funds to localities to take account of the extra cost of special education. Among the different methods of allocating funding to localities, the most common in the late 1990s was through a pupil weighting system under which a pupil with SEN attracts a specified multiple of the cost of a pupil who does not have SEN.

The federal special education law, the Individuals with Disabilities Education Act (IDEA), was reauthorized in 1997, and amendments included changes to funding provisions. One aim is to shift away from funding according to the number of pupils requiring special education towards factors such as the total number of pupils in the area (so-called census-based funding) and the percentages in poverty. Another is to discourage placements in what are considered more 'restrictive' environments.

Some states, prior to the passing of the law, had already moved to essentially census-based approaches. This is seen as having several advantages, including that it takes away the incentive for districts to over-identify pupils 'needing' special education. The approach assumes that pupils with different levels of severity of SEN are evenly distributed across the area concerned. Interestingly, California, one of the states which has moved to a census-based system, also commissioned research to establish whether this distribution was in fact even. Regarding pupils with SEN who were 'severe/high cost', the researchers proposed a system of 'severity adjustments' based on previous district practices and fixed for five years to remove any incentive to 'find' greater proportions of pupils attracting higher funding (Bowers and Parrish, 2000).

SEN funding – a case study

A practical approach was one of the virtues of the British general the Duke of Wellington. As he was about to retire to bed and was informed that the ship in which he was travelling was likely to sink, he announced, 'Very well then, I shall not take off my boots.' A similar practicality was the guiding principle of a change to local funding. This case study concerns the allocation of additional educational needs funding according to level of learning difficulty in an English LEA. Schools received funding for SEN in this particular LEA in four elements:

1. Funding for pupils with statements of SEN.
2. Indirect funding through receiving support in different degrees from LEA centrally funded support staff such as educational psychologists, teachers for pupils with specific learning difficulties and so on.
3. Funding through a formula based on age-weighted pupil numbers.
4. Funding (called additional educational funding: SEN) allocated according to an annual inventory of SEN. This last source of funding applied only to primary schools, as secondary schools already had a system to allocate this additional funding according to scores on a reading test taken in the year that pupils entered the secondary school.

The LEA proposed to re-examine the allocation of the additional funding element for primary schools to try to ensure the fairer allocation of funds. In doing this, the LEA sought to ensure that the greatest level of funding would go the schools having the greatest number of pupils with the greatest levels of learning difficulty.

The difficulty was that funds were allocated according to the number of pupils that each school considered had SEN. Samples of the documentation for each school were collected and checked annually in a process called a moderation exercise. However, the process did not moderate in the sense that it sought to ensure comparability among the pupils identified at different levels of the *Code of Practice* (that is, with different levels of severity of learning difficulties).

The pupils were identified by each school as having a particular level of SEN in line with the *Code of Practice*. However, the school could determine this level with reference only to other pupils in the school. In other words, the judgement of the level of SEN and the number of pupils at each level was contextual to the school. In addition to this, each school received increased funding the more pupils with SEN it had. This was an incentive for schools to identify increased numbers of pupils with SEN. Furthermore, even schools in which pupils achieved at high levels (for example, in terms of National Curriculum levels) could claim that they had a high percentage of pupils with SEN because the attainment of the pupils so identified was some way behind that of other pupils in the high-performing school. This combination of contextual judgements within each school and financial incentives for greater numbers of pupils with SEN was considered by the LEA to lead to an unfair allocation of funds.

A small 'funding group' of LEA officers, headteachers and SEN coordinators was convened to seek a fairer system. After considering various models, including ones adopted by other LEAs, the group recommended the following methods of allocating funds.

1. A common baseline assessment of reading made when pupils were five years old was used to determine the funding for pupils in years 1 and 2. Pupils scoring in the lowest 25 per cent of the baseline reading scores attracted funding.
2. National Curriculum test results in reading taken at the end of Key Stage 1 (the National Curriculum stage when the pupils are seven years old) were used to fund years 3, 4, 5 and 6. Pupils would normally be expected to reach level 2 of the National Curriculum at the end of Key Stage 1, so the funding was allocated to pupils who scored level 1 and below. More specifically, funding for year 3 was based on the National Curriculum results in the previous year (that

is, when these pupils took the test at the end of Key Stage 1). Funding for year 4 was based on the results of the pupils' National Curriculum tests two years previously. Year 5 funding was determined by the National Curriculum test results three years earlier and year 6 funding was worked out according to the results of National Curriculum tests four years previously.

After identification of the pupil numbers for each year group that attracted funding, these were added together to give the total number for each school. The grand total of pupils to attract funds in all schools was then calculated. The sum of money that was to be allocated to all schools was then divided by the number of pupils to receive funding. This gave the funding per pupil. This was to be distributed to each school according to the number of pupils in the school who attracted the additional funding.

Once this was worked out, an issue had to be addressed concerning the possible 'double funding' of schools with pupils for whom English was an additional language. The SEN additional funding focused on low attainment. But it was not practicable to gather information relating to slow progress which would have helped to confirm that the pupils concerned were likely to have SEN. Consequently, some of the pupils would be likely to be those for whom English was an additional language who may have had low standards of attainment in English reading but may not have been making slow progress. Therefore, the SEN funding group recommended that a formula was worked out to try to ameliorate the possibility of double funding by taking into account the numbers of pupils in each school for whom English was an additional language. For schools whose budget would be greatly reduced by the new approaches to funding, transitional arrangements were considered to reduce the funding to fairer levels, but in a phased way.

When available figures were analysed for the year in which the budget changes were first considered, the percentage of pupils found to fall below level 1 of the National Curriculum at the end of Key Stage 2 was 20 per cent. This compared favourably with the percentage considered manageable. This new funding arrangement was still only a proxy indicator of SEN to make funding fairer. It did not seek to estimate the (relatively small) numbers of pupils who experienced behavioural, emotional and social difficulties, for example. However, such pupils, once the school identified them, were usually supported by a centrally funded group of teachers with particular expertise in these difficulties.

SUMMARY

This chapter has considered the increasing costs of SEN, outlining the national and local allocation of funds in England and Wales. Statements of SEN represent the response in England and Wales to the most severe SENs. The difficulties with school-based contextual judgements of SEN are that they can provide incentives for the identification of pupils with SEN. There are therefore advantages in having more objective criteria for SEN.

A continuum of provision for SEN can be determined according to more objective criteria, and some government documents in England and Wales have been concerned with this. The arrangements for funding SEN in the USA indicate that this country is grappling with similar concerns to those in England and Wales. In the case study relating to the themes of the chapter, an effort was made to relate funding equitably to levels of SEN in schools in a local education authority in England.

It is important that resources are directed to the areas of greatest need. This level of 'need' is expressed in terms of the level of learning difficulty that a pupil experiences and in terms of the degree of disability that hinders access to learning and the curriculum.

Level of learning difficulty is indicated by rate of progress and consequently the standards of achievement a pupil has reached. Therefore, funding is most fairly allocated if it is dispersed with reference to standards of pupil achievement for at least an element of the funding. This is most appropriately done according to agreed and consistent local criteria. If schools determine what they perceive as their own level of SEN within the school context, especially where this attracts funding, this can offer a perverse incentive and act against parity.

References

Barber, M. (1997) 'Target setting and school improvement – the way forward'. Letter to all chief education officers in England, 21 July.

Bowers, T. and Parrish, T. (2000) 'Funding of special education', in M. J. McLaughlin and M. Rouse (eds) *Special Education and School Reform in the United States and Britain*. London: Routledge.

Clarke, C., Dawson, A. and Millward, A. (eds) (1995) *Towards Inclusive Schooling*. London: David Fulton.

Coopers and Lybrand (1996) *The SEN Initiative: Managing Budgets for Pupils with Special Educational Needs*. London: Coopers and Lybrand.

DfE (1994) *The Code of Practice on the Identification and Assessment of Special Educational Needs*. London: Department for Education.

DfEE (1997a) *Excellence in Schools*. London: Department for Education and Employment.

DfEE (1997b) *Excellence for All Children: Meeting Special Educational Needs*. London: Department for Education and Employment.

DfEE (1998) *Meeting Special Educational Needs: A Programme of Action*. London: Department for Education and Employment.

DfEE (2000) *SEN Code of Practice on the Assessment of Pupils with Special Educational Needs*. London: Department for Education and Employment.

DfEE (2000b) *SEN Thresholds: Good Practice Guidance on Identification and Provision for Pupils with Special Educational Needs* (Consultation Document). London: Department for Education and Employment.

Farrell, M. (1997) *Special Education Handbook*. London: David Fulton.

Fletcher-Campbell, F. (1996) *The Resourcing of Special Educational Needs*. Slough: National Foundation of Educational Research.

Kilfoyle, P. (1997) *Every Child is Special: Proposals to Improve Special Needs Education*. London: Labour Party.

OFSTED (1996) *Setting Targets to Raise Standards: A Survey of Good Practice*. London: Office for Standards in Education/Department for Education and Employment.

Parrish, T. (1997) *Special Education Finance*. Washington, DC: Federal Resource Centre for Special Education.

Qualifications and Curriculum Authority (1997) *Baseline Assessment Scales for Children with Special Educational Needs: Teachers' Guide*. London: QCA.

Schools Curriculum and Assessment Authority (1997a) *Value Added Indicators for Schools*. London: SCAA.

Schools Curriculum and Assessment Authority (1997b) *Target Setting and Benchmarking for Schools: Consultation Paper*. London: SCAA.

Schools Curriculum and Assessment Authority (1997c) *Baseline Assessment Scales*. London: SCAA.

Teacher Training Agency (1997) *Consultation Paper on National Standards for Special Educational Needs Co-ordinators*. London: TTA.

US Department of Education (1997) *Nineteenth Annual Report to Congress on the Implementation of the Individuals with Disabilities Education Act*. Washington, DC: USDoE.

CHAPTER 6

The use of SEN standards and progress data with pupil information

Introduction

The richness and credibility of information is important for establishing and sustaining verisimilitude in literature. In the gothic novel *Dracula*, Bram Stoker creates credulity and even plausibility by presenting a variety of data to reveal his tale. Jonathan Harker's journal, various letters, newspaper cuttings and even Dr Seward's phonograph diary all come together to reveal the terrible story. In education, as well as literature, rich and varied data are valued. They need careful handling and a cautious interpretation, and are best viewed along with other information to try to show the fullest picture.

Chapters 6, 7 and 8 all concern data on the standards of achievement and progress of pupils with SEN. Each looks at how data within an individual school on the standards and progress of pupils with SEN might be examined and used.

The present chapter examines how standards and progress data on pupils with SEN may be informed by other information relating to the pupils themselves. These factors may be fixed (like gender) or currently fairly clear (like age or social background). The exception is the pupil's main learning difficulty. This may cease to be a significant enough learning difficulty to be appropriately considered a SEN in certain circumstances. For example, if provision is good enough the pupil would be expected to make sufficient progress for the learning difficulty to be reduced sufficiently to be met in class without individualized approaches or assessment.

Chapter 7 considers how standards and progress data on pupils with SEN may be interpreted in the light of information relating to comparatively fixed and predictable school provision. This includes the quality of teaching of particular teachers and the systems that support and enhance teaching, school organization (including staff roles and responsibilities) and pupil organization (including whole-school and class organization).

In Chapter 8, we look at how standards and progress data on pupils with SEN might be interpreted in the light of comparatively variable provision. This encompasses interventions from professionals, usually external to the school (such as educational psychologists, advisers and inspectors, and speech and language therapists), classroom support from parents and support from members of the local community.

The three forms of data are treated separately to make explanations easier. Some of the data considered in Chapter 6 are fixed (such as gender), while the provision considered in Chapters 7 and 8 is present because of choices made within the school. The data relating to 'variable' provision (Chapter 8) are less reliable than those for more 'predictable' provision (Chapter 7). Therefore, variable data should be treated more cautiously.

The information which is the concern of each chapter can be considered together and may interact. While it is usually necessary to draw out data separately, the wider consideration of various sources of information and how they might influence one another is more likely to give a fuller and more comprehensible picture.

Pupil data on standards and progress

The present chapter, as already explained, concerns how standards and progress data on pupils with SEN may be informed by other data relating to the pupils themselves. Such information may form part of the basic data that the school gathers on its pupils who are identified as having SENs.

The first and most important step is to have data on pupil standards and progress. If the learning difficulty is specific learning difficulty or moderate learning difficulty, particularly important data are likely to be those on the standards of reading of the pupil and progress in reading assessed over a specified period of time. In fact reading is a central issue to SEN generally. A key question asked in a consideration of SEN in a publication from the Centre for Policy Studies is 'can SEN pupils read?' (Marks, 2000, p. 23). If the example of reading difficulties is taken, each pupil with SEN will have a score indicating standards of reading, and if parallel tests are made over a period of time there will also be an indication of progress.

Should the pupil have behavioural, emotional and social difficulties, the data may be an assessment of the personal and social skills that the pupil demonstrates. This might be recorded in the form of a teacher observation schedule completed in a certain period, such as a week, and then added to subsequently to indicate any progress. If the pupil has a dis-ability, such as a visual or hearing impairment, the achievement data are still central as an indication that steps taken to enhance the pupil's access to learning and the curriculum are effective.

Examining standards and progress data in relation to other pupil factors

The next step is to consider pupil factors that might have a bearing on standards and progress of pupils with SEN. An OFSTED (2000a) publica-tion outlines several groups that may be distinguished when looking at education inclusion. These include: girls and boys; minority and faith groups; travellers, asylum seekers and refugees; pupils who need support to learn English as an additional language; and pupils with SEN. They also include: gifted and talented pupils; children 'looked after' by the local authority; other children, such as sick children, young carers, chil-dren from families under stress, pregnant school girls and teenage mothers; and pupils who are at risk of disaffection and exclusion. Where pupils are identified as having SEN, there are sub-groups that can be identified within this group that justify closer examination. Here we look at the following sub-groups as examples:

- gender;
- ethnicity;
- main learning difficulty;
- social background;
- age.

Such factors are often considered in relation to the standards of achieve-ment of all pupils. The approach here is simply to consider them particu-larly for pupils identified as having SEN. If such factors are considered to have a possible influence on all pupils then it is especially important to try to tease out any impact they might have on pupils with SEN, where any data that may help to show how achievement may be raised are valuable.

Examining standards and progress data in relation to gender

Gender differences, real or attributed, have for a long time kept wits busy. Margaret Turnbull the American writer stated that 'When a man con-fronts catastrophe on the road, he looks in his purse – but a woman looks in her mirror.' On the other hand a proverb has it that 'A woman needs a man like a fish needs a bicycle.' Perhaps Vittorio Gassman, the Italian actor, was right when he said, 'Men don't understand women and women don't understand men. And it's better that way.'

In general there is little information on gender and SEN for England. Data for Wales, from the annual census of schools, indicate that in 1998 in all schools 70 per cent of Statements were for boys (11,800), while 30 per cent were for girls (4,900) (Welsh Office Statistical Directorate, 1999, Table 12).

With regard to standards and progress at the school level, if we take the example of gender, the data on, say, reading standards would be set out so that the scores for boys and girls could be compared. The average rate of progress of boys and girls could also be scrutinized. Let us assume that in a particular school the figures for pupils with SEN whose main learning difficulty concerns reading are set out according to gender. The figures for the current standards in reading indicate that boys score significantly lower than girls. The average progress over perhaps six months is then considered by deducting previous scores from current scores and separating the figures for boys and girls. This indicates that the average progress of boys is lower than that for girls.

Issues arising from the data in relation to gender
Regarding the data on boys' and girls' reading standards and progress, the next step is to examine possible influential factors. Among these may be that the resources used capture the interest of girls more than boys. The gender composition of staff (perhaps particularly influential staff or senior staff) may be predominantly female, so boys with SEN do not have male role models in the school. Out-of-school or lunchtime clubs for reading may be attracting predominantly girls. There may be a tendency in the school for boys to regard reading as uninteresting or unappealing.

Possible school responses
Once the school has examined the plausible reasons for the data on reading, it can consider the possible provision to address the apparent discrepancies between boys and girls. What might this be?

The school could review the resources used, auditing those appealing to boys and finding out what materials boys would find more interesting. It could then plan the relocation of resources or the purchase or loan of other resources to address this issue. Long-term staffing policy could aim within the law on equal opportunities to recruit more male members of staff, particularly in senior positions. In the short and medium term, the school could ensure that visiting staff or others, such as artists, sculptors or storytellers, include male role models. If parents helping at the school are mainly or exclusively mothers, the school could examine ways of attracting fathers. The reasons why out-of-school or lunchtime clubs for reading attract predominantly girls could be examined, and strategies developed to interest boys and retain their membership. The factors behind the tendency in the school for boys to regard reading as uninteresting or unappealing could be explored by speaking with boys and seeking ways to engage their interest.

Ethnicity: data, issues and responses

Turning to the issue of ethnicity, the data on reading standards would be set out so that the scores for pupils of different ethnic minorities could be compared. The groupings should not be numerous as otherwise it will be difficult to draw even the most tenuous conclusions. The data might initially consider pupils who are not from an ethnic minority and compare these with all pupils from ethnic minority groups considered together. The average rate of progress of ethnic minorities and others could also be compared.

Let us assume that the figures for pupils with SEN whose main learning difficulty concerns reading are set out according to ethnicity. The figures for the current standards in reading indicate that pupils from ethnic minorities score significantly lower than other pupils. Further analysis indicates that the average progress of the ethnic minority group is lower than that of others.

Next possible influential factors can be examined. Resources may not capture the interest of pupils from ethnic minorities. The staff (perhaps particularly influential or senior staff) may be predominantly not from ethnic minorities. Consequently, ethnic minority pupils with SEN would not have role models in the school. Out-of-school or lunchtime clubs for reading may be attracting predominantly pupils not from ethnic minorities.

This information may encourage a range of possible responses that the school would need to assess and evaluate according to its own circumstances. There could be a review of resources to ensure that they are appealing to pupils with SEN of different ethnic backgrounds. The school could re-examine recruitment procedures. It could explore the potential for employing professionals from ethnic minority backgrounds to contribute to the curriculum, perhaps as visiting specialists such as storytellers or drama workshop leaders. General strategies for improving the attainment of pupils from ethnic minorities are outlined in a recent report by OFSTED (2000b).

Main learning difficulty: data, issues and responses

Turning to the issue of main learning difficulty, the data on reading standards would be set out so that the scores for pupils of different main learning difficulties could be compared. The data might consider pupils who have behavioural, emotional and social difficulties as their main learning difficulty, and compare these with all other pupils with SEN. The average rate of progress of pupils with behavioural, emotional and social difficulties and other pupils with SEN could also be compared.

Assume that the figures on reading standards are set out according to behavioural, emotional and social difficulties. The figures for the current standards in reading indicate that pupils from the group having behavioural, emotional and social difficulties score significantly lower than other pupils with SEN. The average progress of the group with behavioural, emotional and social difficulties is also found to be lower than that of the other pupils with SEN.

Next, other possible influential factors may be examined, among which may be the following. Resources may not capture the interest of pupils with behavioural, emotional and social difficulties. Staff may be less skilled in dealing with pupils with behavioural, emotional and social difficulties than with pupils with other learning difficulties. Because of their difficulties, pupils with behavioural, emotional and social difficulties may be less welcome at out-of-school or lunchtime clubs for reading, and when they attend such activities could be less able to participate.

This information may encourage a range of possible responses that the school would need to assess and evaluate according to its own circumstances. A review of resources could be carried out to improve their appeal to pupils with behavioural, emotional and social difficulties. Training could improve staff skills in dealing with pupils with behavioural, emotional and social difficulties. Extra support could be provided for pupils with behavioural, emotional and social difficulties in out of school or lunchtime clubs for reading. Programmes could be developed to help the pupils to participate more when they do attend such activities. A review of the timetable could help to ensure that sufficient time is spent on personal and social development for all pupils, but particularly those with behavioural, emotional and social difficulties whose personal and social development is behind that of other pupils.

Social background: data, issues and responses

People's occupations sometimes single them out for ridicule or teasing. W. C. Fields said of his own profession, 'Show me a great actor and I'll show you a lousy husband. Show me a great actress and you'll see the devil.' Thomas Campbell, the poet, once excused himself for proposing a toast to Napoleon Bonaparte at a literary dinner and at the same time revealing his views of a profession by declaring, 'Gentlemen, you must not mistake me. I admit that he is the sworn foe of our nation, and, if you will, of the whole human race. But gentlemen, we must be just to our

enemy. We must not forget that he once shot a bookseller.' The occupa-
tion of a child's parents is also a basic indicator of the child's social
background and can have a bearing on the child's education.

If we take the example of social background, the data on reading
standards would be presented so that the scores for pupils of different
social backgrounds could be compared. The categories might be pupils of
parents from professions compared with pupils whose parents performed
manual jobs or were unemployed. The average rate of progress of the
groups could also be compared. If the school does not already have access
to this information, then it will need to consider the ways in which this
might be gathered and its potential usefulness.

Once the figures for the reading standards of pupils with SEN are set
out according to social background, those for the current standards in
reading may indicate that the pupils whose families are manual workers
score significantly lower than the pupils of professional parents. Further
analysis indicates that the average progress of pupils of manual workers
is lower than that of pupils whose parents are professionals.

The next step is to examine possible influential factors. Among these
may be that the resources used capture the interest of pupils from more
privileged families. The values conveyed by staff may signal lower expectations for pupils from less privileged families. Out-of-school or lunchtime clubs for reading may be attracting predominantly pupils from more
privileged backgrounds.

Once the school has examined the possible reasons for the data on
reading, it may be apparent what provision could address the discrepancies between social groups. This might mean reviewing resources to
ensure that they capture the interest of pupils from different social backgrounds. The school could explore ways in which values expressed by
staff can convey high expectations for all pupils and seek ways in which
out-of-school or lunchtime clubs for reading could attract pupils from all
social backgrounds.

Age: data, issues and responses

Age is the font of much humour. The composer Daniel-François-Esprit
Auber recognized that 'Ageing seems to be the only available way to live
a long time', while the actor and singer Maurice Chevalier on a similar
theme admitted, 'I prefer old age to the alternative.' But age is also an
important factor in assessing education.

If we take the example of age, the data on reading standards would be
set out so that the scores for pupils of different ages could be compared.
The average rate of progress of pupils at different ages could also be
compared. The expectation would be that, all other factors being equal,

the standards would rise with increasing age. Progress would be expected to be steady for each age group. If the figures for pupils with SEN set out according to age indicate any trends different from expectations this would need to be explored.

Among possible influential factors are resources capturing the interest of one age group more than others. Out-of-school or lunchtime clubs for reading may be attracting predominantly pupils of certain age ranges and not others. One age group may be receiving more support or more skilled support than another.

Next the school can consider the possible provision which may address the apparent discrepancies between different age groups. It could consider the resources used, auditing ones appealing to particular age groups and finding out what materials the less interested age groups would find more stimulating. The school could then plan the relocation of resources or the purchase or loan of other resources to address this issue. The school could explore the reasons why out-of-school or lunchtime clubs for reading attract predominantly certain age groups and develop strategies to interest and retain the membership of other age groups too. It could review support procedures to help to ensure that support by staff most experienced in SEN is allocated appropriately to pupils of all ages.

Information other than reading scores

In the above examples, looking at gender, ethnicity, main learning difficulty, social background and age, the assumption has been that reading scores are used to determine the respective standards and progress of the various groups.

It will be clear that it would be equally easy to use numeracy scores or the scores from tests and assessments of speaking and listening. Equally, assessments of behaviour, emotional development and social skills could be used, perhaps with the support of an educational psychologist. Other assessments could be utilized, depending on the purpose of the data collection. The main point is that the data demonstrate the standards and progress of pupils with SEN. They also crucially enable the school to look more closely at various sub-groups within the wider group of pupils with SEN to examine whether there are further factors inhibiting standards of achievement and progress.

Schools may decide to take advice from the LEA if they are maintained schools or from other sources regarding the use of information and communications technology to simplify information gathering and its use. The school may also consider seeking advice on the interpretation of the statistics that are produced.

SUMMARY

This chapter considered standards and progress data on pupils with SEN using the example of reading standards. It looked at how this may be informed by other data relating to the pupils themselves, including gender, ethnicity, main learning difficulty, social background and age. While each factor may raise particular issues it is possible to identify a common approach, relating the factor concerned to pupil attainment and comparing different groups.

The model is to analyse data, seek possible reasons to explain the data which relate to school provision and seek to adjust provision to optimize the performance and participation of pupils with SEN. This approach may be used in analysing the standards and progress of all pupils but is particularly important for pupils who have learning difficulties. Various data on standards can be used as well as assessments of reading, including speaking and listening, numeracy and behavioural, emotional and social development.

References

Marks, J. (2000) *What Are Special Educational Needs? An Analysis of a New Growth Industry*. London: Centre for Policy Studies.

OFSTED (2000a) *Evaluating Educational Inclusion: Guidance for Inspectors of Schools*. London: OFSTED.

OFSTED (2000b) *Raising the Attainment of Ethnic Minority Pupils: School and LEA Responses*. London: OFSTED.

Welsh Office Statistical Directorate (1999) *Special Education in Wales*. Statistical Brief SDB 7/99, January. Cardiff: WOSD.

CHAPTER 7

The use of SEN standards and progress data for 'stable' school provision

Introduction

It is not always easy to establish what is stable and what is transitory. The short stories of Somerset Maugham proclaim a world in which the British Empire and its values would live for ever and far-flung outposts such as Borneo would be set in aspic, with prahus passing downstream past Dyak houses. In education it is possible to make a distinction between the stable and the transitory, but one cannot be certain that the categories will hold for long.

In this chapter, the use of data on standards and progress is considered in relation to 'stable' school provision. This provision is that which is characterized by being comparatively longer term, predictable and within the school's control. Among such factors are quality of teaching and school organization.

The quality of teaching is considered, along with the way it relates to provision for pupils with SEN. Particular attention is given to learning support assistants and to the systems and structures supporting teaching. This leads to a consideration of a pupil's access to the curriculum and to the ways in which teaching enhances this.

School organization is considered as it applies to staff and pupils. Staff organization includes roles and responsibilities, staff allocation and in particular the role of the SEN coordinator. The organization of pupils includes the grouping of pupils within usual class groups, the wider organization of pupils into sets, bands, streams and other groupings and the degree to which pupils are withdrawn from lessons or are supported in the classroom. Other organizational features are considered, such as the allocation of staff and the possible effects on standards of pupils with SEN. The chapter considers how these might be addressed.

Quality of teaching
A model to assess the quality of teaching

US journalist H. L. Menken may have taken the need for a lack of discrimination too far when he declared, 'Love is the delusion that one woman differs from another', for discrimination is necessary in many areas and the quality of teaching is one of them. Among the models of what constitutes good teaching and learning is that developed in England and Wales by the Office for Standards in Education (OFSTED, 1999a,b,c), which is based on research into school effectiveness and school improvement.

In determining their judgements inspectors consider the extent to which teachers demonstrate certain qualities, skills and knowledge. These include demonstrating good subject knowledge and understanding, shown through the way they present and discuss their subject. Teachers should be competent in teaching basic skills, including phonics. They should plan effectively. This includes setting explicit and clear learning objectives that pupils understand. They should challenge and inspire pupils and have high expectations of them. A concomitant of this is that pupils should develop deeper understanding and knowledge. Good teachers use methods enabling all pupils to learn effectively. They manage pupils well and make sure they insist on high behavioural standards. Resources are effectively used, including time, support staff and other resources. Good teachers assess pupils' work thoroughly. Assessments are used to assist pupils in overcoming difficulties. Homework is used to reinforce what has been learned in school or to extend school learning.

The handbook of guidance to inspectors makes explicit the rather obvious connection which is expected between teaching and achievement, stating: 'Teaching is fundamental to the quality of education provided by the school and is the main avenue through which the school contributes to pupils' attainment, progress and attitudes' (OFSTED, 1999b, p. 47).

A more recent study reinforcing many aspects of the OFSTED model was developed from teacher interviews and other sources (DfEE, 2000). Reinforcing this are developments following the government Green Paper *Teachers Meeting the Challenge of Change* (DfEE, 1998), which heralded proposals for a threshold leading to performance-related pay. Annual appraisal taking account of pupil standards and linked to pay increases would apply to all teachers. These proposals were carried forward by a document on teacher appraisal published a year later (DfEE, 1999). Implementation of the system began in 2000.

It follows, and it is of course widely accepted, that, all other things being equal, an important way of judging good teaching is through the standards which pupils reach and the progress they make. This is not as straightforward when one is considering pupils with severe disabilities. Subtle professional judgement has to be brought to bear in such cases.

Standards for the award of Qualified Teacher Status (QTS) (Teacher Training Agency, 1998a) apply to all trainees seeking QTS who were assessed from May 1998. To be successful, candidates on initial teacher training courses must achieve all the QTS standards. Courses must assess all trainees against all the standards set out in the awards of QTS.

An important feature of the standards for the award of QTS is that they form a basis for future professional development. These include development through links with the other standards in the professional framework for subject leaders (Teacher Training Agency, 1998a) and headteachers (Teacher Training Agency, 1998c). The strongest thread running through recent developments relating to teacher and headteacher professional development and training is that of standards. This reflects the focus on standards achieved by pupils, and perhaps it is inevitable that a similar attention is given to the standards reached by teachers and headteachers in various roles.

Teaching pupils with SEN
Related to this are developments in setting standards for SEN coordinators (Teacher Training Agency, 1998b, 2000) and specialist standards (Teacher Training Agency, 1999).

The *National Standards for Special Educational Needs Co-ordinators* (Teacher Training Agency, 1998b) sets out the core purpose of the SEN coordinator (SENCO), the key outcomes of SEN coordination, professional knowledge and understanding, skills and attributes, and key areas of SEN coordination. In many parts of the document there are less precise references to meeting needs, with no indication of what this would mean or how it would be known if needs were met. Elsewhere, however, there are more purposeful references to standards and access.

Among the key outcomes for SEN coordination are that pupils on the SEN register 'show improvement in literacy, numeracy and information technology skills' and that such pupils are 'helped to access the curriculum'. While teachers should be familiar with and implement 'approaches to meeting the needs of pupils with SEN', learning support assistants should become knowledgeable in 'ways of supporting pupils and help them to maximise their levels of achievement and independence' (p. 6).

In professional knowledge and understanding, the SENCO should have knowledge and understanding of, among many other things, 'the main strategies for improving and sustaining high standards of pupil achievement' and (in collaboration with the information technology coordinator, how IT 'can be used to help pupils gain access to the curriculum' (p. 8).

Key areas of SEN coordination include that SENCOs 'support staff in understanding the learning needs of pupils with SEN and the importance of raising their achievement' (p. 12). SENCOs also should 'support the development of improvement in literacy, numeracy and information technology skills, as well as access to the wider curriculum' (p. 13).

To take another example, in the *National Special Educational Needs Specialist Standards* (Teacher Training Agency, 1999) the core standards refer to the development of literacy, numeracy and information and communication technology (ICT). The skills and attributes required of teachers working with pupils with severe or complex SEN indicate the importance of raising standards of pupil achievement.

The same principles of good teaching apply to all pupils, including those with SEN, and it is therefore reasonable to judge teaching according to the progress of pupils with SEN. It may be that such pupils start from a lower starting point than the average in, say, reading or mathematics, but the progress and the subsequent standards reached can be used as an indication of teaching quality.

In assessments of the quality of teaching, the contribution of learning support assistants is often an important factor. The work of the teacher (who assumes overall responsibility for the learning of pupils) with the learning support assistant can be judged according to the extent to which it improves standards of pupil achievement. Factors such as clear shared learning objectives, shared planning and monitoring by the teacher of what the pupils with SEN have learnt are important.

Linking quality of teaching and curriculum access

Access to the curriculum involves ensuring that what is offered to pupils is, as far as can be reasonably expected, taken up by them. A key part of helping to ensure this is through the teacher using methods enabling all pupils to learn effectively. This involves matching the work closely to the prior attainment of pupils; that is, 'differentiation'.

Differentiation is centrally related to differences in attainment. It concerns the closest matching of activities and the capabilities of pupils. Differentiation is a planned process of organization and intervention in the classroom aiming to ensure that school work is well matched to the individual characteristics of pupils. It concerns pupils of all abilities and is consequently a whole school concern. Differentiation involves:

- a variety of teaching and learning styles which build on the interests and experiences of all the pupils in a classroom;
- matching the task to the learning needs of the pupils;

- linking planning, learning and teaching into a cycle to identify and match tasks to needs;
- recognizing individual entitlement and access to the National Curriculum (National Curriculum Council, 1993).

The effectiveness of differentiation can again be usefully judged according to its impact on standards of pupils with SEN.

Systems supporting and enhancing the quality of teaching

The nature of an activity cannot be properly understood unless the structures around it are known. This principle is used to comic effect by Dickens, for example, in *Oliver Twist*, where Oliver, newly arrived in Fagin's house, is easily confused by the 'work' of the Artful Dodger and Charlie Bates. Referring to two pocket books that the Dodger has stolen, Fagin says to Oliver, 'Ingenious workman, ain't he Oliver?' Of Bates's acquisition of 'wipes', Fagin asks Oliver if he would be able to make pocket handkerchiefs 'as easy as Charlie Bates'. Both comments greatly amuse the boy pickpockets.

The activity of teaching is of course not just the task itself, but also the structures that surround and support it. One of the ways in which teaching is supported and enhanced is by agreed planning systems. These may involve ensuring that long- and medium-term curriculum and subject plans include tasks and assessments enabling pupils with SENs to reach the learning objectives required.

A related way in which systems support teaching is by ensuring that the resources required for the teaching are sufficient in quantity and in quality. This may mean for pupils with SEN the use of specialist resources. Yet another is the system of monitoring the effectiveness of teaching and ensuring that teachers are aware of the weaknesses and strengths of their teaching. Teachers may be given written reports of their teaching, with weaknesses and strengths clearly identified and targets for improving the weaknesses set. Reaching these targets may involve support and training and perhaps the provision of physical resources. These support systems again can be assessed according to their impact on raising achievement.

In England and Wales, performance management arrangements are being introduced in which the career progression and pay of teachers will be partly determined by the progress made by the pupils whom they teach.

Comparing teaching provision

If the data collected on pupils with SEN are comprehensive, comparisons of progress can be made according to the main teacher working with the children. In the primary school where pupils spend much of the day with the same teacher this may be done by comparing the standards of pupils with SEN who started from a similar point but are in different classes. For example, the standards and progress of two cohorts of five or six pupils with similar levels of reading difficulties could be compared in different classes. With such small numbers, such a comparison would not of course stand statistical scrutiny. But if the two cohorts of pupils appear to have similar levels of difficulty and one cohort is progressing much better than the other, it is fair to question why.

In upper primary school and in secondary school, where teachers teach particular subjects, other comparisons can be made. The progress of pupils with SEN who have difficulties in English and mathematics could be compared. If the progress was different in different subjects this could be explored. The general progress of pupils with SEN could be tracked to see which pupils were progressing satisfactorily and which were not (and why).

All these approaches are not necessarily intended to lay blame at the door of a particular teacher but to identify, in the same way as for pupils in general, what is working for pupils with SEN and what is not. It essentially involves making use of data in the same way as for all pupils, but with the focus on the cohort of pupils that have SEN, or a sub-group of that cohort.

School organization
Staff and pupils
Through the organization of its staff and pupils the school increases or decreases the ability of the school to raise the pupils' standards of achievement. Part of staff organization is the roles and responsibilities of staff, including their communications. The organization of pupils refers to the grouping of pupils within usual class groups and the wider organization of pupils into sets, bands, streams and other groupings.

Staff roles and responsibilities
An underlying principle in teaching pupils with SEN is that of providing the greater level of support to those with greater 'need'. A manifestation of this is that the school aims to set up systems which help to ensure that staff with the greatest level of skill or expertise are deployed with the pupils who most require their time.

In England and Wales, it is expected that the class teacher of a pupil will make the initial judgement about whether a pupil has SEN. While this is daunting for the newly qualified teacher particularly, in each school the presence of a SENCO, a teacher with particular expertise in

SEN, acts as a safeguard. From the earliest indications of SEN, the class teacher may consult with the SENCO for advice, support or practical help. If the pupil does not make expected progress, the SENCO becomes progressively more involved. Should the skills of the SENCO not increase progress, the school may call on outside support as necessary. This may be from an educational psychologist, a speech and language therapist, a physiotherapist, a behaviour support teacher and so on. This approach also applies to greater amounts of time being spent with pupils who have greater learning difficulties. In brief, then, the intention is to enhance the likelihood of achievement being raised by focusing increasing levels of expertise and time on the pupil according to his or her lack of progress.

Some difficulties of staff allocation

Sometimes schools may focus very well on allocating extra time to pupils with SEN, but may not always focus commensurate expertise or experience on the pupil's difficulties. The increasing use of learning support staff is open to this weakness. Many support staff work with individual pupils or small groups for a considerable part of the pupil's timetable. They often provide a valuable contribution to the pupils' education. Where the learning support assistants are ineffectively or inappropriately used, the child can effectively be denied the skills and knowledge of the teacher. At the same time, the teacher may be gradually losing the skills he or she might have in providing for pupils with SEN.

This may be particularly marked in the case of pupils with emotional and behavioural difficulties. The pupil becomes increasingly dependent on the individual teaching provided by the learning support assistant and less and less able to respond in a whole-class setting. Simultaneously, the teachers may be losing skills in dealing with difficult behaviour. The level of achievement of the pupils in the development of personal and social skills is likely to be lowered.

Among the ways of reducing the potential disadvantages of these arrangements is to ensure that the teacher, as well as the learning support assistant, devotes sufficient time to pupils with SEN and that the teacher and learning support assistant have time to share planning based on clear learning outcomes. The teacher can also monitor these learning outcomes during the lesson.

The role of the SENCO

To excel at one's chosen profession requires dedication and hard work. The violinist Pablo Sarasate was called a genius by a music critic and responded, 'For thirty seven years I've practised fourteen hours a day, and now they call me a genius!'

The role of the SENCO may or may not require genius but certainly it is complex and demanding, not least because others' expectations of the SENCO may be conflicting (Farrell, 1998). National standards for SENCOs illustrate the demands of the role (Teacher Training Agency, 1998a, 2000), making the importance of raising the standards of pupil achievement and increasing progress clear. The national standards for SENCOs comprise five parts:

- the core purpose of the SENCO;
- key outcomes of SEN coordination;
- professional knowledge and understanding;
- skills and attributes;
- key areas of SEN coordination.

The core purpose of the SENCO is to 'bring about improved standards of achievement for all pupils'.

The key outcomes of SEN coordination include that pupils on the SEN register 'show improvement in their literacy, numeracy and information technology skills', that teachers have 'high expectations of pupils' progress' and that learning support assistants help pupils to 'maximise their levels of achievement and independence'. In the area of professional knowledge and understanding, the SENCO should have knowledge and understanding of 'strategies for improving and sustaining high standards of pupil achievement'. Turning to skills and attributes, these do not explicitly refer to standards and progress.

Four key areas of SEN coordination are set out: strategic direction and development of SEN provision in the school; teaching and learning; leading and managing staff; efficient and effective deployment of staff and resources. Strategic direction and development includes the need for the SENCO to support staff in understanding 'the importance of raising ... achievement'. The SENCO also advises the headteacher and governors on the level of resources needed to 'maximise the achievements of pupils with SEN'.

Pupil organization

As indicated above, the organization of pupils refers to the grouping of pupils within usual class groups and the wider organization of pupils into sets, bands, streams and other groupings. This includes the degree to which pupils are withdrawn from lessons or are supported in the classroom.

Whole-school organization

The effect of the school's organization at the whole-school level into structures such as sets, bands and streams may be monitored for all pupils. It may become clear that a judgement about setting is improving overall standards. However, the same analysis is not always done with respect to pupils with SEN as a group, where the effects of organizational structures on standards may not be the same as they are for all pupils taken together. It may be that the effects of an organizational feature are detrimental to the standards and progress of pupils with SEN. If so, then the reasons can be explored and action taken to maintain possible positive effects on the standards of all, at the same time as ensuring that the standards of pupils with SEN increase also.

Classroom organization
If pupils are withdrawn from the classroom for support, the effects of this may be monitored and compared with the standards and progress of pupils with similar levels of learning difficulties supported within classes. The reasons for any differences in progress can be hypothesized and possible rearrangements to the existing systems may be made using evidence from the school and its own particular circumstances.

The use of standards and progress data in relation to school organization
Perhaps the most useful approach to using standards and progress data to appraise school organization is through benchmarking with similar schools. A school may be making better progress, and therefore raising standards of pupils with SEN, than another similar school. The similarity may be based on the fact that the schools have a similar cohort of pupils with SEN and are similar in other respects, such as the quality of teaching offered. If other factors appear equal, this could encourage the school whose performance with its pupils with SEN is less good to review its organizational arrangements for such pupils.

There are various areas that the school might review. The allocation of time to pupils with SEN could be considered to ensure that any extra individual time was based on levels of learning difficulty or disability. The school should be able to ensure that the level of expertise and skill that is directed towards different pupils with SEN is related to learning difficulty and degree of disability. There should be built-in and organized opportunities for communications within the school, including joint planning between teachers and learning support assistants. The structure for bringing expertise and skill to bear on pupils with SEN within the school should be reliable and robust. The training of staff in SEN, in particular for newly qualified teachers and teachers new to the school, should be rigorous. The SENCO should be effective in the coordinating role to ensure timely and appropriate intervention. The organization of pupils with SEN, including the degree to which pupils are withdrawn from lessons or are supported within lessons, should also be effective.

The school's response will depend on the outcomes of such a review and on the particular factors thought to be affecting standards and progress. Suitable responses may therefore be various. The school may improve its identification and assessment procedures and better equate these with the level and quality of intervention made. The school may ensure that all staff are trained to deliver what is expected and that the staff with the greatest expertise are deployed where they are most effective.

Securing and monitoring the built-in and organized opportunities for communications, including joint planning between teachers and learning support assistants, is also important. The school could improve the reliability and robustness of the structure for bringing expertise and skill to bear on pupils with SEN within the school through matching staff skills more closely to pupils' learning difficulties. For example, this could be done by ensuring that staff who are trained in working with pupils with visual impairments in the school are optimally deployed with those pupils.

The school could review and develop staff training in SEN, in particular for newly qualified teachers and teachers new to the school, through the use of in-school or out-of-school in-service training and education. It could ensure that the SENCO coordinates effectively to ensure timely and appropriate intervention through making this expectation explicit in the job specification and allocating time for this to be done. The school could closely monitor the effects on academic and personal and social standards of pupils in relation to the organization of pupils with SEN, including the degree to which pupils are withdrawn from lessons or are supported within lessons, and adjust the balance of provision accordingly.

SUMMARY

The use of data on standards and progress was considered in relation to 'stable' school provision. This stable provision is comparatively longer term, is predictable and is within the school's control.

The quality of teaching and the way it relates to provision for pupils with SEN was considered, with particular attention paid to learning support assistants and to the systems and structures supporting teaching. This led to a consideration of a pupil's access to the curriculum and the ways in which teaching enhances this.

Pupil organization included the grouping of pupils within usual class groups, the wider organization of pupils into sets, bands, streams and other groupings and the degree to which pupils are withdrawn from lessons or supported in the classroom. Other organizational features were considered, such as the allocation of staff and the possible effects on standards of pupils with SEN and how these might be addressed.

References

DfEE (1998) *Teachers Meeting the Challenge of Change.* London: Department for Education and Employment.

DfEE (1999) *Performance Management Framework for Teachers.* London: Department for Education and Employment.

DfEE (2000) *Research into Teacher Effectiveness. Report by Hay McBer to the Department for Education and Employment.* London: Department for Education and Employment.

Farrell, M (1998) 'The role of the special educational needs co-ordinator: looking forward'. *Support for Learning,* **13**(2), 82–6.

National Curriculum Council (1993) *An Introduction to Teaching Geography at Key Stages 1 and 2.* London: NCC.

OFSTED (1999a) *Handbook for Inspecting Primary Schools with Guidance on Self-evaluation.* London: The Stationery Office.

OFSTED (1999b) *Handbook for Inspecting Secondary Schools with Guidance on Self-evaluation.* London: The Stationery Office.

OFSTED (1999c) *Handbook for Inspecting Special Schools and Pupil Referral Units with Guidance on Self-evaluation.* London: The Stationery Office.

Teacher Training Agency (1998a) *National Standards for Qualified Teacher Status, Subject Leaders, Special Educational Needs Co-ordinators and Head Teachers.* London: TTA.

Teacher Training Agency (1998b) *National Standards for Special Educational Needs Co-ordinators.* London: TTA.

Teacher Training Agency (1998c) *National Standards for Head Teachers.* London: TTA.

Teacher Training Agency (1999) *National Special Educational Needs Specialist Standards.* London: TTA.

Teacher Training Agency (2000) *Using the National Standards for Special Educational Needs Co-ordinators.* London: TTA.

CHAPTER 8

SEN standards and progress data for 'variable' school provision and the role of documentation

Introduction

In Dickens's *Hard Times*, Thomas Gradgrind, in teaching children, wants only facts, facts, facts. He wishes to plant nothing else and root out everything else. But facts and data need not be dry. Indeed, they are part of the life-blood of a school.

Regarding school data, the term 'variable' is used here simply to convey those aspects of school provision less under the control of the school than, for example, the quality of teaching and the whole-school and within-classroom organization. The variable aspects include 'external' professional support and the contributions of parents and the community. This chapter considers how the use of data on SEN standards and progress may inform the support provided by professionals and lay people. It also outlines the role of standards in school documentation, including Individual Education Plans and school SEN policies.

Professional support

Educational psychologists, advisers and inspectors, speech and language therapists, the peripatetic SEN specialist teacher, physiotherapists, behaviour support staff, drama therapists, art therapists and many others will contribute to raising the academic or personal and social achievement of pupils. The contribution of each can be viewed through this context.

To take educational psychologists as an example, a report on their current role and future aspirations (DfEE, 2000) sets out their 'core functions'. These include working with pupils either individually or in groups and working with schools. Schools want, among other things, school-based work in behaviour management. LEAs want psychologists to provide preventative work on avoiding social exclusion. Among the recommendations are that educational psychologists' roles should be clear. Within all this it should not be too difficult to identify ways of working that some of the time can be demonstrated to raise pupil achievement.

For instance, a psychologist in liaison with the school might intervene in a more timely way at levels of SEN not requiring the issuing of a Statement. If so, does this over a year or so in a particular school appear to aid the raising of standards when compared with earlier approaches which focused more on pupils with Statements?

Data on pupil achievement may be considered in relation to such professional interventions. This is likely to involve good measure of professional judgement. However, it is reasonable to ask, after, for example, an educational psychologist's input into a behaviour modification programme, to what degree the programme and the psychologist's input have contributed to raised achievement in the pupil's personal and social development. In other words, the school and others can judge how successful the intervention has been.

Sometimes the contribution of professionals who support the school may be at one remove. For example, an adviser or inspector may introduce the school to a resource such as a piece of computer software, which may lead to some pupils making better progress than they might have otherwise in a certain area of the curriculum. Or they may train staff through in-service education in a particularly effective approach to teaching mathematics. Nevertheless, it is reasonable to try to track the contribution to raising pupil attainment.

Possible questions for the school to raise if the intervention appears ineffective are:

- Do partners share the school's awareness of the task of raising achievement?
- Are all partners aware of the range of approaches used by the school to raise achievement, and the contribution they can make?
- Does the support or advice that was offered represent good value for money?
- How long do school staff spend working with partners and does the 'return' justify this time?

Having considered these questions, the school may not be certain of the value of the interventions. If it is judged that the contribution of professional support colleagues is not sufficiently raising levels of achievement of pupils, possible school responses are as follows.

- All partners should be made aware of the range of approaches used by the school to raise achievement and the contribution they can make.

- Can the school agree with partners on the strategies, including teaching and learning strategies, that will raise achievement?
- If value for money is low, are there other sources of similar advice or support that might offer better value for money? 'Fair funding' approaches taken by local authorities in England and Wales involve local councils being aware of the sources of competition for the services they offer to help to ensure that they provide value for money. This introduces an element of market competition into the services that schools can use and is intended to lead to more efficient services.
- Can the time spent by the staff of the school working with partners be reduced and still lead to the same results, thereby possibly improving value for money?

Naturally, it does not have to be only the school that considers matters from this perspective. Supporting professionals may themselves seek to evaluate their contribution in terms of its effect on raising standards of pupil achievement. These professionals and the schools with which they work may develop a shared perspective of raising standards that could be expressed as part of a service-level agreement.

Parents

Quentin Crisp, the late writer and one-time art model, said, 'If one is not going to take the necessary precautions to avoid having parents one must undertake to bring them up.' A similar thought expressed by novelist Anthony Powell was, 'Parents are sometimes a bit of a disappointment to their children. They don't fulfil the promise of their early years.' Whatever the limitations of parents, they are key partners in the effective education of their children.

Among developments underlining the importance of parental involvement in the education of their children are parent partnership schemes. The Green Paper *Excellence for All Children* (DfEE, 1997) argues that local SEN parent partnership schemes have helped LEAs to work more effectively with parents whose children have SEN, especially those who are undergoing statutory assessment or who have a Statement of SEN. The government proposed to extend such schemes through a form of targeted funding, the Standards Fund. A parent partnership scheme might involve a voluntary body as well as the LEA and parents. It could:

- offer a resource and information base for parents and professionals working with children with SEN;
- help to provide training;
- recruit, train and support 'named persons' to assist the parents of children with SEN (DfEE, 1997, Chapter 2).

The *Programme of Action* (DfEE, 1998) stated that from 1999 government would expect each LEA to have a parent partnership scheme. The scheme would ensure that the parents of any child identified as having SEN should have access to an independent supporter.

Each school should carefully develop its own policy for parental involvement so that partnership can be based on agreed roles and responsibilities. Parents may be involved in the school setting targets for their son or daughter and may contribute to the achievement of the target through supporting the pupil's work carried out at home. Home–school agreements or contracts can help to clarify the respective roles of parents and teachers in this area. Parents may also give crucial support in helping a pupil to reach behavioural targets. Of course, it is a valuable motivating factor for many pupils for them to see that the school and home are working together for their benefit.

When parents help in class it is reasonable to ask to what degree they are contributing to raising standards. It is said that in a classroom in London, a grandmother of one of the pupils in the school was helping the teacher by hearing children read and, it was assumed, assisting them. The school was visited by a school inspector who realized very quickly that the grandmother could not herself read. The school had apparently assumed that the presence of another adult was a given good, and had not considered the importance of the impact on pupil achievement (or in this case the lack of it). Of course, this example is extreme, but it is clear to teachers that some parents with particular skills are likely to raise standards, while others are not.

Possible school responses if it is judged that the contribution of parental support is not sufficiently raising levels of achievement of pupils are:

- ensuring that parents and the school agree on the importance of raising standards and the strategies for doing so;
- improving the contribution of parents through brief sessions of training, perhaps provided by the school;
- putting in place a tactful screening procedure for recruiting parents from those who have volunteered to help.

The community

Writers sometimes portray the community as if it were something quite separate from them. H. L. Mencken thought that democracy was 'The theory that common people know what they want, and deserve to get it good and hard.' More pointedly, Oscar Wilde, speaking of journalism, said, 'There is much to be said in favour of modern journalism. By giving us the opinions of the uneducated, it keeps us in touch with the ignorance of the community.' A less amusing but more generous and realistic perspective on the community is as a body to which we all belong and from which a school as part of this community can often draw goodwill and support.

Links with the community, including higher education and business, can be viewed as a given good, but can also be informed by the effect on attainment. Links with local universities or colleges of further and higher education may be used to recruit mentors for some pupils with SEN who could benefit. Business contacts may include those with companies who could provide resources for pupils with SEN at a competitive rate or free. The effect on standards of achievement should be trackable, if only in a fairly anecdotal way. The data may show that some human and physical resources had a more beneficial effect on standards of achievement than others.

Questions arising from an analysis of the data may include the following.

- Are the learning resources that did not work well sufficiently well targeted, appealing and motivating?
- What is it about effective volunteers that distinguishes them from the less successful?

This information might be used to:

- feed information back to companies to improve the appeal and interest of their learning resources;
- inform the recruitment and the in-school training of volunteers.

Documentation

School records often include a basic list of pupils with SEN, their main learning difficulty and the provision planned to address it. More detailed records are often variations of individual plans which set out more precisely, among other details, what is being done to address the learning difficulty, how its success will be judged and the timescale of the interventions.

An important aspect of school record-keeping is that it should make clear the standards of achievement and progress of pupils with SEN. Records should be used not just to record but to assist in modifying approaches and in confirming that the provision is successful.

Transition from primary school to secondary school

Record-keeping in relation to pupils who are changing schools is important in helping to maintain special school standards. Such records include those for pupils with SEN transferring from primary to secondary school. Information sharing should involve a system of meetings with colleagues from secondary schools to discuss issues and particular children. Documents need to be passed on at an agreed time, with an agreed content and in an agreed way (by hand or by e-mail). If the information sharing is monitored, this will help to make sure that it happens and may give pointers to how to simplify and improve procedures. Parents should be involved and made aware of the contacts between primary and secondary school. In their final year at primary school pupils benefit from being able to visit the secondary school which they will attend, for a tour and/or to experience a lesson there. The secondary school will probably have its own induction system and may choose to open only for year 7 pupils on the first day of the new school year.

Year 7 teachers in secondary schools may consider that they receive insufficiently detailed information on pupils entering year 7 to inform their planning. However, the outcomes of the National Curriculum assessments at the end of Key Stage 2 appear to be insufficiently used to ensure the smooth progress of pupils moving from year 6 to 7. Locally, schools need to agree the dates in the summer term when assessment data will be transferred. Schools should agree what will be included: raw test scores, age-standardized scores, separate levels for reading and writing and teacher assessment judgements relating to attainment targets. Timing and good quality information are important to enable secondary schools to use the information to inform their decisions about the grouping of pupils. All this applies to all pupils (Farrell, 2001) but is likely to be particularly helpful to ensure timely and appropriate provision for pupils with SENs.

Individual Education Plans

A John Lennon lyric speaks of life being what happens to you while you are busy making other plans. This reinforces the truth that what matters is not so much the planning (and certainly not the written plan) but what goes into the planning process and what stems from it. However, to ensure clarity of purpose and to avoid duplication of effort, as well as for other reasons, plans can be useful.

In England and Wales, for pupils with SENs, an Individual Education Plan (IEP) is normally maintained. This sets out the SEN of the pupil, the provision intended to address them and individual targets to aim for within a specified time frame. For example, for a pupil with numeracy difficulties, a target might be to be able to compute a specified list of mathematical problems with 90 per cent accuracy within six weeks, through half an hour per day individual tuition on similar types of problems.

If raising standards and improving progress is seen as central to special education, then it follows that IEPs should contribute to raising achievement in a clearly specified way. The strategies specified in IEPs would draw on the range of approaches set out in the school SEN policy and contribute to reaching group targets for pupils with SEN. The sharing of targets with the pupils to whom they apply may help the pupils achieve the target, particularly if they have had an input into setting the target in the first place.

There is a drawback with IEPs, however. It is difficult to know if the individual targets set in IEPs are sufficiently ambitious for a particular pupil. Judging the appropriate combination of target and the timescale for achieving it for an individual pupil sets a challenge for even the most experienced teacher. It cannot be known securely whether the targets set in IEPs are sufficiently stretching or are quite unchallenging. If targets of numeracy progress were set for pupils on the register of SEN, these could be much more advantageously compared with the progress which pupils make in similar schools having a similar number of pupils on their register at similar levels. This benchmarking of schools according to the levels of achievement would concentrate on pupils requiring a focused individualized approach.

Another perspective would be to aim for sufficient progress to be made by a pupil in numeracy in, say, a year, so that his achievement would be such that it would no longer represent the cohort of the low percentile that it did on the previous testing. If sufficiently rapid progress was made, this might indicate that the child does not have SEN but 'only' low attainment. At the same time, the new assessment level would be likely to lift the pupil out of the cohort that would be considered to have SEN, or SEN at a particular place in the framework of the SEN Code (for example, 'school support' or 'support plus'). If slow progress were made then the reverse would be indicated. It would suggest that the child had SEN. The SEN might also need to be addressed through a more intensive level of support; for example, 'support plus' rather than 'school support'.

The SEN policy

In England and Wales, it is an expectation that mainstream schools (and special schools) have a policy of SEN. While this can be at its least useful a rather bland document, it can at its best be used to galvanize and focus support both from outside the school and within it.

The school's SEN policy may be used as a tool to assist in the raising of standards of achievement. For example, the standards of all pupils or groups of pupils with SEN may be determined, with targets set for the improvement of standards of achievement in a specified time, e.g. six months. Strategies for achieving this improvement would also be specified.

The policy would set out the range of strategies used by the school and might include: a reading recovery programme, the use of new resources, focused work with a member of staff for a specified period per week, a behaviour modification strategy and so on. The overall success or otherwise of the strategy would be monitored and evaluated. Such group target setting, if well judged, can raise the aspirations of staff and pupils higher than they might otherwise be, in the same way as whole-school target setting for all pupils.

The standards achieved by pupils with SEN can be used to evaluate different approaches, such as the differential use of withdrawal from class or working with pupils within class. If both approaches are used, it may be feasible for the school to compare pupils beginning from a similar starting point but who receive one approach as opposed to another. All other factors being equal, this could indicate the effectiveness of one approach over another at that time in the school's development. If these analyses are informed by the financial cost of different approaches, the information can indicate the value for money of one approach compared with another.

The raising of achievement may be monitored and evaluated in an ongoing way by the senior management team in a school and by individual teachers. Governors will also be able to monitor the raising of standards if the information relating to this is put before them at the relevant meetings.

Support to schools may come from locally provided professional support or from parents and representatives of the local community, including business. Such support may be usefully evaluated in the SEN policy according to the degree to which it is judged to have raised standards of pupil achievement.

SUMMARY

The contribution of professional and lay support can be judged according to the degree to which it raises the standards of pupil achievement. Steps can be taken to improve the effect of this support on pupil achievement.

Turning to documentation, school records should make clear the standards of achievement of pupils with SEN and their progress. Documents should be used not just to record but to provide evidence to modify approaches and confirm that the provision is successful.

Transition from primary school to secondary school is important for all pupils, but with pupils with SEN there is a particular opportunity to ensure as smooth a transition as possible. Among approaches to assist this are locally agreed strategies for what information is to be transferred, when and how it is to be transferred and to what use it will be put.

There are limitations to the effectiveness of Individual Education Plans in raising standards and increasing progress unless their use is informed by other measures, including the utilization of data from a cohort of pupils with SEN. Among the limitations of IEPs are that it is difficult even for teachers regularly in contact with pupils to be confident that the targets are sufficiently ambitious to be challenging. The school's SEN policy should be a dynamic working document pulling together the strategies used to raise the standards of pupils with SEN and monitoring the effectiveness of these approaches.

References

DfEE (1997) *Excellence for All Children: Meeting Special Educational Needs*. London: Department for Education and Employment.

DfEE (1998) *Meeting Special Educational Needs: a Programme of Action*. London: Department for Education and Employment.

DfEE (2000) *Educational Psychology Services (England): Current Role, Good Practice and Future Directions*. Report of the Working Group. London: Department for Education and Employment.

Farrell, M. (2001) *Key Issues for Secondary Schools*. London: Routledge.

CHAPTER 9

The special school

Introduction

Wartime British prime minister Winston Churchill observed, 'When I look back on all these worries I remember the story of the old man who said on his death bed that he had had a lot of trouble in his life, most of which had never happened.' Staff in good special schools may be forgiven if they are worried about the future of the pupils whom they teach, given some comments made in the debate on inclusion. Among these are the statement in the Green Paper on special education in England and Wales (DfEE, 1997, p. 43) that there are 'strong educational as well as social and moral grounds for educating children with SEN with their peers'.

In recent years, in part because of increased interest in aspects of inclusion, the role of the special school has come under critical scrutiny. It is important that the function of the special school be fully understood and agreed. This can help to enable fair judgements to be made about the continuation and the evolving role of individual special schools on educational grounds, and not inordinately according to any political ideology. Standards of achievement have a key role to play in this judgement (Farrell, 2000).

A more balanced view of the role of the special school is likely to appear when two developments occur. First, supporters of full inclusion will need to come to recognize the work that good special schools achieve. Second, those who would wish to see special schools continue only on ideological grounds, rather than on merit, will need to recognize that special schools must earn their place in the range of effective educational provision. Until then proponents of full inclusion and those who work in special schools are likely to be like film director Woody Allen's lion and calf. 'The lion and the calf shall sleep together but the calf won't get much sleep.'

Definitions

The definitions of SEN are as relevant to the special school as to the mainstream establishment. Special schools are often designated as providing for pupils with particular SEN, although in many special schools the SEN are complex and cannot be adequately described solely with reference to one main SEN (such as behavioural, emotional and social difficulties). Nevertheless, special schools focus on a main area of SEN, such as: severe learning difficulties/profound and multiple learning difficulties; behavioural, emotional and social difficulties; moderate learning difficulties; communication and interaction; sensory and physical.

Just like mainstream schools, special schools (and others) will bring definitions to bear in their admissions procedures. This definition may involve seeking to specify a degree of severity of SEN that will explain why a pupil is offered a place in a special school rather than a mainstream school. The definition may include a description of the complexity of the SEN, as well as its degree of severity. Standards of achievement have their place in this situation to the extent that some SEN are defined according to learning difficulty (severe, profound, moderate). Admission will also be influenced by parental preference, the effective use of resources and the effect that admission to a mainstream school would be judged to have on other children in a mainstream classroom.

Identification and assessment

It has long been accepted that special schools would normally provide for pupils with the greatest 'need'. This can be seen as providing for pupils with:

- the greatest level of learning difficulty evidenced by pupils who make the slowest progress and consequently attain the lowest standards without intensive support and specialist provision;
- the greatest degree of disability.

In England and Wales, this level of learning difficulty is normally associated with a quasi-legal document, a 'Statement of SEN'. Consequently, special schools normally provide for pupils with Statements, although some offer assessment places to pupils who do not have such Statements. Over half the number of pupils with Statements of SEN are educated in mainstream schools.

Curriculum, assessment and target-setting

In special schools, there are tensions around the curriculum, as a study of special school inspections in England and Wales illustrated (Sebba *et al.*, 1996). On the one hand, special schools may be expected to provide a broad and balanced curriculum, in England and Wales including the National Curriculum. On the other hand, they may more effectively raise achievements by focusing on other features. These include:

- the 'access' subjects of English, mathematics and information technology, which, as well as being important in themselves, allow access to other subjects and areas of the curriculum;
- personal and social education.

Similar issues arise with regard to assessment. If the curriculum of a special school differs too greatly from that of a mainstream school, then assessments will need to be modified so that they focus on what has been taught. For example, if there is a concentration on functional skills such as eating, washing and dressing, these will need to be assessed. It is important that such curriculum developments are dovetailed into the wider agreed National Curriculum for all children.

Within special schools it is difficult to compare pupils meaningfully for the purpose of target-setting. Among the reasons for this is that different special schools may have similar designations but may not have similar pupils. For example, consider two special schools in different areas, both providing for secondary age pupils with behavioural, emotional and social difficulties. In one local area there may be a unit in one or more mainstream secondary schools which serve such pupils, while in the other there may not. In one district, it may be more likely that pupils with very severe difficulties are placed in residential schools elsewhere; in the other, it may be much more likely that the local schools would be expected to provide.

Such examples can be extended both for pupils with behavioural, emotional and social difficulties and for those with other SEN. The outcome is that the intake of the special school may not be similar, making comparisons difficult. It is important to ensure therefore that when one is looking at outcomes such as standards of achievement in apparently similar schools, the cohort of each school can be fairly compared.

In England and Wales, where pupils are working at levels below the National Curriculum level 1, among the approaches taken to assess pupils is the use of the p scales. These are performance criteria with elements for language and literacy, mathematics and personal and social development (DfEE, 1998b). They have been found to be useful for pupils with severe learning difficulties and for some pupils with moderate learning difficulties. An example of an item on the p scales is in language and literacy – writing, in which item 4 is:

pupils make marks or symbols in their preferred mode of communication and are beginning to show an awareness that marks or symbols

convey meaning, e.g. generating a symbol from a selection on a computer, painting/drawing/making a mark on paper. (DfEE, 1998b, p. 26)

A few practical examples can illustrate the way in which target-setting
may be tackled.

In a primary school for pupils with severe learning difficulties/profound
and multiple learning difficulties (SLD/PMLD), it was decided that setting
statutory targets was unproductive. This is because targets at level 2 and
above in the National Curriculum tests for English and mathematics at the
end of Key Stage 2 give percentages year on year of 0 per cent owing to the
nature of the pupils' learning difficulties. More relevant were targets con-
nected to the work done within the organization Equals, a consortium of
schools for pupils with SLD/PMLD. A national database for pupils with
SLD/PMLD was set up in the latter part of 1999, enabling the school to
compare itself with similar schools so that target-setting and benchmarking were more meaningful. This approach has been related to the development of a curriculum and an associated scale of assessment. These scales
have been used to assess more than 3,000 pupils in over 160 schools for
pupils with SLD/PMLD. Results were used to provide comparative data,
allowing benchmarks to be made against the whole cohort and targets to
be set in individual schools according to their profile compared with the
whole cohort of pupils. Each school was able to compare pupils that were
in upper, middle and lower performing bands within the school.

A secondary school for pupils with SLD/PMLD also felt reservations
concerning statutory targets. The school set targets in terms of the percentage of pupils who achieved some form of accreditation and improved
attendance. It is actively seeking ways to represent standards of attainment based on existing accreditation used in the school.

In a primary school for pupils with MLD the special educational needs
of the pupils mean that the percentage of pupils achieving national
curriculum level 4 and above in English and mathematics at the end of
Key Stage 2 would be 0 per cent year on year. Consequently, targets have
been set relating to the percentage of pupils achieving level 2 and above
at the end of Key Stage 2.

A secondary school for pupils with MLD recognized that the special
educational needs of the students meant that none would achieve one of
the statutory targets: five or more A* to C grades in the GCSE examinations. However, there are pupils who achieve one or more GCSEs A* to G,
which is another statutory target, and the school's targets are set in these
terms.

A primary school for pupils with behavioural, emotional and social
difficulties has set targets in terms of the percentage of pupils in year 6

achieving level 4 and above at the end of Key Stage 2. However, this has to be seen in the context of the very small cohort and the special educational needs of the pupils. The school is also more effectively using the results of reading tests and a mathematics test taken by all pupils to set targets in terms of increases in knowledge and skills year on year.

At a secondary school for pupils with behavioural, emotional and social difficulties, targets have been set in relation to the percentage of pupils who achieve one or more GCSEs and to the percentage who achieve Certificates of Educational Achievement, which underpin GCSEs.

Inclusion and the 'new' role of the special school

In the Green Paper *Excellence for All Children* (DfEE, 1997, p. 49), the traditional role of the special school was seen as providing, 'specialist teaching, support and facilities'. The document recognizes the continuing need for special schools to provide for a very small proportion of pupils whose needs cannot be fully met in mainstream. In some cases this provision would be temporary. The Green Paper also envisaged a new role for special schools. It was proposed to examine how special school staff could work more closely with mainstream schools and with support services to meet the needs of pupils with SEN. Staff in special schools 'might work in resourced mainstream schools or in units attached to mainstream schools' (p. 50). Special schools could also set 'targets for the amount of time pupils should participate in mainstream education' (p. 51).

In special schools some pupils would be in full-time placements, while others would be there part-time or short term. Special school staff could:

- support some pupils in mainstream;
- help mainstream schools to implement their policies for inclusion;
- train and advise mainstream colleagues (p. 51).

Government wanted 'real progress over the next four years' (that is, from late 1997 to 2001).

The document *Meeting Special Educational Needs: a Programme of Action* (DfEE, 1998) sets out the intention to promote further inclusion and develop the role of special schools through measures including 'identifying and disseminating good practice by special schools in developing practical links with mainstream schools, and promoting special schools' contribution to an increasingly inclusive educational system' (p. 22).

'Special provision' would continue to play a vital role. Such provision would often be in special schools but not always (p. 23). There would be no local and national targets for inclusion but government would keep under review their possible value. Special schools would need increasingly to 'work flexibly' (p. 25).

As indicated in the earlier chapter on inclusion, standards can be used to help to inform judgements about the appropriateness or otherwise of a placement in a special or a mainstream school. It is essential therefore that special schools know what their standards of achievement are and can set data relating to this beside data on standards reached by broadly comparable pupils in local mainstream schools. This is not to imply a rigid distinction between the special and mainstream school.

An important role for the special school is to identify with others the pupils in the school who will benefit most from proportions of time in mainstream schools with a view to increasing the proportion of time in the mainstream if progress is made. Special schools may also have close links with units in mainstream schools working with pupils with the same main SEN. Such units can act as a bridge to aid the gradual transfer of a pupil from special to mainstream school, judged according to progress made and standards of achievement reached.

Funding

Arnold Schwartzenegger, the film actor, made the observation, 'Money doesn't make you happy. I now have $50 million but I was just as happy when I had $48 million.' The importance of funding is at the forefront when one scrutinizes what special schools offer. Being an expensive form of provision makes it important that special schools can demonstrate the progress that they enable pupils to make and the levels of achievement which pupils can achieve from a known starting point. Their contribution as a centre for the training of staff, for physical resources and advice, as well as for outreach work, also adds to the value for money that a special school can provide.

The use of SEN standards and progress data with pupil information

To balance against the common view of data and statistics as ingenuous, it is well to remember the comment of Noel Moynihan, the doctor and writer: 'Statistics can prove anything, even the truth.'

Information on special schools judged in inspections by the Office for Standards in Education in the years 1994 to 1998 were summarized in a subsequent report (OFSTED, 1999). In the years before 1996/7, standards in special schools were judged in terms of pupil attainment in relation to their capability (although it was unclear how 'capability' was judged). It was recognized that in most special schools it was not fitting to judge pupil attainment against the national norms.

After the introduction of a new Framework for Inspection in 1996/7, standards in special schools were judged in terms of pupil progress.

Again it is difficult to know how it can be judged whether progress is satisfactory. The report recognized the difficulties posed by the change in the basis of judgement part way through the inspections summarized (p. 9). However, the report stated that with reference to special schools, 'during the first three years of the review standards were rising slowly' (p. 11). In schools inspected in the final year (1997/8), 'standards were higher' (p. 16). Pupils made satisfactory or better progress in nine out of ten special schools – a proportion similar to that of progress in mainstream.

However, there were greater proportions of weak special schools than there were mainstream schools. The report recognizes the importance of standards of pupil achievement, although there are difficulties in its findings, and not just because of the change of criteria in the final year of the inspections reported. Other difficulties are the problematic nature of making judgements about standards in relation to 'capabilities' that anyone would find difficult to estimate. Also problematic is the issue of making inspection judgements about standards in relation to progress, when expected progress is also very difficult to estimate, even for teachers who work with pupils for long periods.

The analysis of standards and progress data and pupil factors may cover gender, ethnicity, main learning difficulty, social background and age. All of these apply to special school analyses. In the case of some SEN, the interpretation of gender data requires caution because there are gender factors associated with the SEN. For example, in autism, there are three times as many boys as girls affected. Rett Syndrome and Turner's Syndrome affect girls only.

But whereas a mainstream school is advised to monitor the standards achieved by its cohort of pupils with SEN, the special school would be advised to make particular note of the progress of sub-groups of pupils within the main SEN for which it provides. For example, a school for pupils with severe learning difficulties could monitor the progress and standards of pupils who also have autism or those who have particular difficulties with communication. The point of this monitoring would be to establish the progress and achievement, to look for difficult to explain anomalies and to use these to seek ways of further improving provision and therefore raising standards.

The use of SEN standards and progress data for 'stable' school provision

In the inspection report on special schools in England from 1994 to 1998 mentioned above (OFSTED, 1999), the quality of teaching in special schools was judged to be satisfactory or better in nine out of ten special schools in the year 1997/8. There were variations according to the main learning difficulty for which the special school provided, with generally lower levels of teaching quality in schools for pupils with emotional and behavioural difficulties.

The quality of teaching in a special school can be judged against agreed criteria such as those published by OFSTED in England and Wales. It can also be evaluated according to the progress made by pupils in different class groups, as long as it is clear that comparisons are justifiable and fair.

Turning to curriculum access, within a special school there may be predominantly provision for a particular aspect of SEN, such as behavioural, emotional and social difficulties or visual impairment. Nevertheless, there will also be a range of prior learning and the need to meet the learning needs of a diverse population. This makes effective differentiation just as important as in a mainstream school. School organization, the deployment of staff and the grouping of pupils are clearly as important in a special school as in a mainstream school.

The use of SEN standards and progress data for 'variable' school provision

The same approach that is recommended for mainstream schools regarding judgements of the effectiveness of professional and lay support can also be used by special schools. Indeed, it can be argued that it is even more important that a special school knows the value of support, as it gets so much more than a mainstream school.

The special school's use of human resources often has economies of scale and can demonstrate the best use of time. For example, fifty pupils with severe learning difficulties in a special school may also need regular physiotherapy for physical difficulties. Fifty similar pupils may be attending ten different mainstream schools. It is a better use of the physiotherapist's time to work with the pupils in the special school than to spend most of the time travelling from school to school when the pupils are dispersed over several mainstream schools.

SUMMARY

While special schools are often designated as providing for pupils with particular SEN, in many special schools the pupils cannot be adequately described solely with reference to one main SEN. Special schools bring definitions to bear in their admissions procedures, perhaps involving specifying a degree of severity and complexity of SEN that explains placement in a special school.

Standards of achievement are important in admissions, to the extent that some SEN are defined according to learning difficulty.

Special schools normally provide for pupils with Statements of SEN, although some offer assessment places to pupils who do not have such statements.

Within special schools it is difficult to compare pupils meaningfully for the purpose of target-setting; for example, because different special schools may have similar designations but may not have similar pupils. Therefore, when one is looking at outcomes such as standards of achievement in apparently similar schools it is important to ensure that the cohort of each school can be fairly compared.

In England and Wales, where pupils are working at levels below the National Curriculum level 1, among the approaches taken to assess pupils is the use of the p scales and a scale of assessment developed by the organization Equals. Other approaches are being developed by special schools to provide for pupils with other SEN such as behavioural, emotional and social difficulties and moderate learning difficulties.

Standards can be used to help to inform judgements about the appropriateness or otherwise of a placement in a special or a mainstream school. Special schools need to know their standards of achievement and should compare data relating to these with data on standards reached by broadly comparable pupils in local mainstream schools. The special school may also identify the pupils in the school who will benefit most from time in mainstream schools with a view to increasing the proportion of time in the mainstream if progress is made. Special schools may also have close links with appropriate units in mainstream schools to aid the gradual transfer of a pupil from special to mainstream school, judged according to progress, standards of achievement and other factors.

Special schools should be able to demonstrate the progress that they enable pupils to make and the levels of achievement which pupils achieve from a known starting point. Their contribution as a centre for training staff, for physical resources and advice, as well as for outreach work, also enhances value for money.

The analysis of standards and progress data and pupil factors may cover gender, ethnicity, main learning difficulty, social background and age. The special school should also make particular note of the progress of sub-groups of pupils within the main SEN for which it provides. One point of monitoring is to establish the progress and achievement, and to look for difficult to explain anomalies and use these to seek ways of improving provision and raising standards further.

The quality of teaching in a special school in England and Wales can be judged against agreed criteria, such as those published by OFSTED. It can also be evaluated according to the progress made by pupils in different class groups, as long as it is clear that comparisons are justifiable and fair. Within a special school, there may be predominantly provision for a particular aspect of SEN, but there will also be a range of prior learning and the need to address the learning needs of a diverse population. This makes the need for effective differentiation important. School organization, the deployment of staff and the grouping of pupils also importantly relate to standards of pupil achievement.

Special schools need to make judgements of the effectiveness of professional and lay support. The special school's use of human resources often has economies of scale and can demonstrate the best use of time.

References

DfEE (1997) *Excellence for All Children: Meeting Special Educational Needs*. London: Department for Education and Employment.

DfEE (1998a) *Meeting Special Educational Needs: a Programme of Action*. London: Department for Education and Employment.

DfEE (1998b) *Supporting the Target Setting Process: Guidance for Effective Target Setting for Pupils with Special Educational Needs*. London: Department for Education and Employment.

Farrell, M. (2000b) 'Educational inclusion and raising standards'. *British Journal of Special Education*, **27**(1), 35–8.

OFSTED (1999) *Special Education 1994–98: a Review of Special Schools, Secure Units and Pupil Referral Units in England*. London: The Stationery Office.

Sebba, J., Clarke, J. and Emery, B. (1996) 'How can the inspection process enhance improvement in special schools?', *European Journal of Special Needs Education*, **11**, 82–94.

CHAPTER 10

Conclusion

In the introduction to this book, we set out the 'bill of fare to the feast'. It follows that in the conclusion, it only remains to remind diners what has been laid before them. This book in each of its chapters has sought to indicate the importance of standards of pupil achievement in all aspects of special education. Standards (understood as encompassing academic attainment and achievement in other areas, including behavioural, emotional and social development) are important in the definition of many areas of SEN and an indicator that provision is effective in all areas of SEN.

'Learning difficulties' are defined according to standards and progress, and the effectiveness of provision may be judged according to how it increases progress and raises standards. 'Disability' is seen in terms of access to learning and the curriculum. The severity of the disability is judged according to the extent to which it hinders access to learning and the curriculum, while the effectiveness of provision is judged according to the extent to which it aids access.

Curriculum and assessment are potential aids to the education of pupils with SEN, in that they can provide a common framework and a common language for provision and assessment. Extending the lower levels of the curriculum and providing smaller steps to learning enables progress to be made. Assessment accommodations to the general curriculum provide opportunities for pupils with SEN to demonstrate their achievements.

Where different aspects of curricula and different assessments are necessary, these should still be consistent to enable comparisons to be made of pupil standards of achievement and progress. For pupils with SEN the role of standards of achievement is important as the starting point for target-setting, and is central to benchmarking and value added measures. This applies whether the attainment is related to learning difficulties or is a pragmatic indicator of the effectiveness of provision which aims to ensure access to learning and to the curriculum for disabled pupils.

The approach of 'educational inclusion' takes into account the standards reached in different venues (including mainstream school, special school, pupil referral unit and home education) when the appropriate place for a child to be educated is being considered.

Funding is most fairly allocated if it is dispersed according to standards of pupil achievement and agreed and consistent local criteria. If schools determine what they perceive as their own level of SEN within the school context, especially where this attracts funding, this can be a perverse incentive and act against parity.

A useful approach using SEN data to raise standards is to analyse data, seek possible reasons to explain the data which relate to school provision and seek to adjust provision to optimize the performance and participation of pupils with SEN. Various data on standards can be used, as well as assessments of reading, including speaking and listening, numeracy and behavioural, emotional and social development. Other data that can help to raise standards for pupils with SEN include the quality of teaching (and systems and structures that support teaching) and the way it relates to provision for pupils with SEN. Pupil organization and the allocation of staff can be judged and improved through their possible effects on the standards of pupils with SEN.

The contribution of professional and lay support can be judged and improved according to the degree to which it raises the standards of pupil attainment. School records should make clear the standards of pupils with SEN and their progress. These documents should be used not just to record but to modify approaches and confirm that the provision is successful. Transition from primary school to secondary school is assisted by locally agreed strategies. The use of individual education plans should be informed by other measures, including the use of data involving a larger cohort of pupils with SEN. The school's SEN policy should be a dynamic working document pulling together the strategies used to raise the standards of pupils with SEN and monitoring their effectiveness.

Special schools have an important place in the range of provision for pupils with SEN. Various factors related to standards influencing the field of SEN in general also have an impact on special schools. These factors include: definitions of SEN and disability relating to identification and admissions; the curriculum and assessment; target-setting, benchmarking and value added measures; inclusion; funding; the use of SEN standards and progress data (on pupil information, 'stable' school provision and 'variable' school provision).

Standards of pupil achievement permeate all aspects of special education and should be given greater priority than at present to lead to greater agreement in our understanding and approaches. Although Oscar Wilde referred to consistency as 'the last refuge of the unimaginative', he could not possibly have had special education in mind, for it is an area in which a greater degree of consistency than we have at present would be enormously beneficial.

Index